\すぐに役立つ/
オンライン会議の
ビジネス英語
★社内会議編★

寺尾 和子(著)・柳川 史樹(著)

クリステン・ランウンズ (英文編集)

メディカルパースペクティブス

はじめに
一 本書を手に取ってくださった皆様へ

　世界規模のパンデミックの発生により、多くの企業は在宅ワークを導入し、会議もリモートが主流になりました。パンデミックが一段落した後も、Zoom などを活用したウェブ会議が日常茶飯事的に実施されています。

　特に多人数が参加するような英語のオンライン会議では、相手の表情や反応の把握が難しく、また、通信事情によっては音声が聞きづらいなど、コミュニケーションの難易度がさらに高くなってしまいます。

　間違いを恐れずに、主張すべきことは積極的に主張して、納得の行くオンライン会議にするためには、役立つフレーズや言い回しなどを事前に身につけて、準備しておくことが重要と考えます。

　本書では、さまざまなビジネス分野に応用できそうなフレーズを、できるだけ多く選ぶよう心がけました。ですが、これらはあくまでも会話のとっかかりに過ぎません。願わくば、このとっかかりをもとに、よりスムーズに会話が進み、より専門的な領域の議論へ展開していくことを期待しています。

　本書が少しでも皆様のご活躍の一助になれば、これほど嬉しいことはありません。

著者・編集者一同

目 次

第 1 章 導入編 会議開始前の確認・進行全般

第2章 会議編

Coffee Break

第1章
導入編

会議開始前の確認・進行全般

第1章 導入編
会議開始前の確認・進行全般

①会議を始める前の確認

■声が聞こえるかどうか確認する

▶ 皆さん、聞こえますか？

- Can everyone hear me?

▶ （申し訳ありませんが）少し聞こえづらいです。

- (I'm afraid) I'm having trouble hearing you.
- I can't hear you well.

▶ もう少しマイクに近づいて話してくださいますか？

- Could you please come/speak a little closer to the microphone?

▶ もう少し大きな声で話していただけますか？

- Could you speak up a little, please?
- Would you mind speaking a little louder, please?

▶ 音量を少し上げていただけますか？ 音が少し小さいようです。

- Can you please turn up the volume a little bit?
  I think your volume is a bit too low.

  （マイクの）音を大きくする／小さくする
  turn up/down the volume (on the mic)

▶ はっきり聞こえています。

- I can hear you loud and clear.

■参加者が揃ったかどうか確認する

▶ みなさん、揃いましたか？
- Is everybody here?

▶ チームの皆さんは揃っていますか？
- Is everyone here from your team?

▶ 皆さんお揃いですね。
- I think/believe we're all here.

▶ こちらは全員揃いました。
- From our side everyone's ready.
- Everyone's here from our end.
- Our side is all here.

■来ていない人を確認する

▶ 誰がまだ来ていませんか？
- Who isn't here yet?

▶ まだ来ていない人はいますか？
- Is someone not here yet?
- Are we missing anyone?
- Is anyone absent?

▶ 鈴木さんがまだ会議に入っていません。
- Mr. Suzuki hasn't joined us yet.
- Mr. Suzuki isn't here yet.

▶ 鈴木さんはあと 5 分位で参加できるでしょう。
- Mr. Suzuki will be able to join in about 5 minutes.

▶ 彼は 5 分くらい遅れます。
- He's going to be late by 5 minutes or so.
- He'll be about 5 minutes late.

■あと少し待つ

▶ あと数分で始めます。
- We'll get started in a few minutes.

▶ 全員が揃うまでもう少し待ちましょうか？
- Shall we wait a few more minutes until everyone is here?
  ～ until everyone arrives?,　～ until everyone joins?

▶ もう少し待って全員が揃ってから始めましょう。
- Let's just wait a bit more for everyone to join.

 Coffee Break
― 出席をとります！

参加者リストが表示されるようなオンライン会議では不要ですが、そのような機能が利用できない場合の出欠確認の方法。

出席をとります。
- Let me take attendance.

名前が呼ばれたら返事してください。
- Please answer/respond when your name is called.
- I'll call the roll. Please answer when you're called.

出席をとる　take attendance, check attendance
点呼する　take a roll call, do a roll call, call the roll
はい、います！　Here!, I'm here!, Present!
彼女は欠席です。　She's absent.

②会議の開始

■会議を始める

▶ 開始時間になりましたね。
- I think it's time to start now.

▶ 皆さん、今から始めてもよろしいですか？
- Is everybody ready to start (now)?
- Is everyone OK to start?

▶ 始めましょうか？
- Shall we start now?
- Shall we begin?
- Shall we get started?

▶ では、会議を始めます。
- Now, let's get started.
- Now let's get going.
  「早速始めましょう」「さあ（そろそろ）始めましょう」のニュアンスがあります。

▶ 全員揃ったと思いますので、始めましょう。
- I think we're all here, so, let's get started.
- Well, I think everyone is here. Let's start now.

■全員が揃わなくても始める

▶ 時間が迫っているので全員が揃わなくても始めましょう。
- Time is pressing, so, let's start even if we don't have everyone.
  pressing（形）急を要する、（必要性が）差し迫った、

5

③開始の挨拶

■参加を感謝する

▶ ご参加いただきありがとうございます。

- Hello everyone! Thank you for joining/coming.
- I appreciate your attendance (at this meeting).
- I'd like to welcome you all and thank everyone for coming.

▶ お忙しい中、出席してくださりありがとうございます。

- Thank you for taking (the) time out of your busy schedules to attend (this meeting).

   ここの "the" はあってもなくても正解です。もし特定の努力や ヘルプをしてくれた場合は、"taking the time" となります。

   忙しい中、〜のため時間を割く
   take (the) time out of one's busy schedule to 〜

▶ まずは、お忙しい中、お時間を割いて参加していただき ありがとうございます。

- First, I'd like to thank you all for taking (the) time out of your busy schedules to participate.

▶ 集まってくださった皆様に感謝の意を表したいと思います。

- I'd like to express my appreciation to you all for coming.

   〜のために時間を割いてくださったことに感謝します。
   I'd like to thank you for taking the time to 〜
   I appreciate you taking the time to 〜
   〜のために時間を割いてくださったことに感謝の意を表したい。
   I'd like to express my gratitude for taking the time to 〜
   時間を割いてこれを書いていただき、ありがとうございました。
   Thank you for taking the time to write this.

■お会いできて嬉しい（場を和ませる）

▶ 皆さんお元気そうで何よりです。
- I'm glad you're all looking well.
- I'm glad to see everyone looking well.

▶ 皆さんにまたお会いできて嬉しいです。
- It's nice to see everyone again.

■進行係について知らせる

▶ 本日は私、鈴木が進行係（司会進行）を務めさせていただきます。
- My name is Suzuki and I'll be facilitating this meeting.
- I'll be hosting this meeting.
- I'll be the moderator for today's meeting.
- I'll act as the moderator for today.
- I'll host the meeting today.

▶ 本日の進行係は営業部の山本さんです。
- The facilitator for today's meeting is Mr. Yamamoto from the Sales Department.

▶ 最初に、部長のスミス氏から一言ご挨拶をさせていただきます。
- Before we begin/get started, our Director, Mr. Smith, would like to have a few words.

④進行に関する事務的なお知らせ

■発表中、聞き手はミュートに

▶ 最初に、いくつかの事務的なことについてお話しします。

- Just a few housekeeping points/items before getting started.
- Let's start with a little bit of housekeeping.

  housekeeping =「家事」の意味ですが、会議では「事務的なこと」
  の意味でよく使われます。
  housekeeping announcements/issues/matters/points/items

▶ 参加時は全員がミュートになっています。

- All attendees are muted when joining the meeting.

▶ 発表者の話を全員が良く聞こえるように、皆さんは「ミュート」になっています。

- You have been placed on "mute" to ensure all participants can hear the speakers.

▶ 発言したいときはミュートを解除し、話し終わったら、再度ミュートにしてください。

- Please unmute when you wish to speak, and mute (yourself) again when you've finished.

▶ ミュートになっていることを確認してください。

- Please make sure you're on mute.

■ 録音に関する事前確認

▶ 本会議は録音させていただきます。予めご了承ください。

- I'd like everyone to know (in advance) that this meeting will be recorded.

- I'd like to let everyone know in advance that we'll be recording the presentations.
- I'd like to inform everyone in advance that the meeting will be recorded.

  "inform" はフォーマルな響きのある表現です。

■発表時間について

▶ 各発表時間は 10 分です。ご留意ください。

- Each presentation will last 10 minutes. Please keep this in mind.

▶ 各発表者に割り当てられた時間（10 分）を厳守してください。

- Each speaker must strictly adhere to the allotted time (of 10 minutes).
- Please make sure that each speaker sticks to the allocated time (of 10 minutes).

▶ 各発表者に割り当てられた時間は、質疑応答を含めて合計 15 分です。

- The total time allotted to each speaker is 15 minutes, including Q&A.

▶ 決められた時間を守ってください。

- Please follow the time set for the meeting.
- Please follow the meeting timeline.
- Please stick to the schedule.
- Please follow the time limit.

  時間通りに来てください。
  Please be sure to come on time.
  Please be on time.

■質問があればチャットボックスに

▶ 発表が終わるまで皆さんは「ミュート」になっていますが、もし質問がある場合は、チャットボックスに書いてください。

• You'll remain on mute until the presentation ends, but you can ask questions by typing them into the chat box.

▶ 技術的な問題がある場合は、チャットボックスに知らせていただければサポートします。

• If you're having any technical problems, please use the chat box and we will try to assist.

■質疑応答について

▶ 発表後に質疑応答の時間を設けています。

• There'll be time for Q&A after the presentation.

▶ 質問は話を最後まで聞いてからにしてください。

• Please hold your questions until the end.

• If you have any questions you'd like to ask, please leave them until the end.

• Please save any questions until after the presentation.

▶ 質問は発表後までお待ちいただけるとありがたいです。

• I'd be grateful if you could wait to ask your questions until after the presentation.

▶ 各発表の終了時に質問応答に移ります。
- Questions will be addressed at the end of each presentation.

▶ 質問する前にお名前を言ってください。
- Please state your name at the start of your question.

▶ 発表中に質問があればお受けします。
- We'll be open for questions during the presentations.

▶ もし質問があれば遠慮なく中断して聞いてください。
- Please feel free to interrupt if you have questions.
- Don't hesitate to interrupt if you have a question.
- Please stop the presenter if you have any questions.

▶ 不明な点があれば、いつでも質問してください。
- If you need clarification at any point, you're welcome to ask.

▶ 質疑応答では、ご自由に発言してください。
- During the Q&A, please feel free to say whatever you want to say.
- Please don't hesitate to ask any questions during Q&A.

■会議のスケジュールについて

▶ 会議は 2 時間の予定です。
- The meeting is scheduled for two hours.

▶ 会議は 3 時に終わる予定です。
- The meeting will close/end at 3 pm.
- The meeting is scheduled to end at 3 pm.

▶ 2 時から 5 分間の休憩をはさむ予定です。
- There will be a 5 minute break at 2 pm.
- We will take a 5 minute break from 2 pm.

■〜時には絶対に終了しなくてはならない

▶ この会議は 3 時には絶対に終わらねばなりません。
- We have a hard stop (for this meeting) at 3 pm.
- 3 pm is a hard stop (for this meeting).

▶ 私はこの会議後に別の会議があるので、3 時には絶対に終わらねばなりません。
- I have another meeting after this one, so, I have a hard stop at 3 pm.

会議では "hard stop" は、「終了時間の厳守」の意味でよく使われますが、「急停止、突然の停止」や「即座に絶対に終わらせる」ような意味でも使われます。

やむを得ない場合を除き、急停止は禁物です。
Please don't make a hard stop unless otherwise inevitable.

10万ドルを越える取引にはハードストップを設定してあります。
We've placed a hard stop on transactions over US$100,000.

この問題についてはこれ以上議論するつもりはありません。終わり。
I'm not going to discuss this issue any further. Hard stop.

⑤議事録について

■議事録の作成

▶ 本日は佐藤さんが議事録をとります。前述のように全発表と議論内容を録音しますので、ご了承ください。

- Mr. Sato will be taking the minutes today. As mentioned before, the whole presentation and discussion will be recorded. Thanks for your understanding.

  議事録／会議メモをとる（議事録の minutes は常に複数形）
  take minutes/notes
  "meeting minutes" と "meeting notes" はどちらも会議でよく使われますが、"notes" は重要点などを書きとめたメモ（社内会議など）、"minutes" は会議全体を詳細に記録した正式な文書。

  議事録を作成する
  draw up the minutes
  会議の記録（メモ）をとる
  take notes at the meeting
  概要（要約）を作成する
  make a brief summary (of this meeting, of what we've discussed)

▶ どなたか議事録を作成していただけませんか？

- Could somebody take the minutes for us?

■議事録は後日送信

▶ 議事録は後日メールで送信する予定です。

- We'll send the minutes via email later.
- The minutes will be emailed at a later date.

  via email と by email はどちらも使われます。
  via = by way of（〜の方法で、〜を経由して）
  via はよりフォーマルでビジネス的、by はより一般的で日常的

13

▶ 議事録（会議メモ）は作成次第、メールでお送りします。

• **The minutes (notes) will be sent by email as soon as they've been prepared.**

▶ この会議の概要は 1 週間くらいで送信予定です。

• **The summary of this meeting will be sent in a week or so.**

メールに添付して送るような場合は "will be sent by/via email" もしくは "will be emailed"、手渡しで配布されるような場合は "will be handed out"。

■各自メモを取ることを推奨

▶ 今回、特に議事録の作成は予定しておりませんので、必要ならば各自メモを取ることをお勧めします。

• **We're not planning to take minutes for this meeting, so we recommend that you take notes on your own as necessary.**

必要に応じて
as necessary, as appropriate, as needed, if necessary, if needed, if desired, where appropriate

■録音停止について

▶ すみません、雑音が入るので、録音を一旦停止します。

• **Sorry, there's some noise, so I'll stop recording for now.**

▶ 個人的な質問の時は録音を停止します。

• **The recording will be paused during individual questions.**

第２章
会議編

第2章 会議編

①本題に入る・議題・目的（進行係から）

■（前置きはこのくらいにして）本題に入る

▶ 前置きはこのくらいにして、本題に入りましょう。
- So enough introduction, let's get started.
- Enough with the introductions, let's get down to the main topic.

▶ では、本題に移りましょう。
- Now, let's get started.
- All right, let's move on to the main subject.
- Now, I would like to move on to the main topic.

■（時間がないので）本題に入る

時間がない時や重大な会議などで、単刀直入に本題に入る場合の表現

▶ 時間が限られておりますので、さっそく本題へ入らせて
いただきます。
- We don't have much time so I'll get straight to the point.
- Today's meeting is brief, so I'll get right to the point.

▶ **さっそく（単刀直入に）本題に入らせていただきます。**

- **Let me get straight to the point.**

　早く核心に触れてよ！（早く要点を言ってくれ！）
　Get straight/right to the point!
　Cut to the chase!

　単刀直入に言わせてください。
　Let me cut to the chase.

　では、先に進めましょう。
　Okay, moving on.
　Okay, let's move on.

■**アジェンダ（議題）について**

▶ **皆さん、アジェンダのコピーをお持ちですよね？**

- **Everyone has a copy of the agenda, right?**

▶ **メールでお送りした配布資料をお持ちですよね？**

- **You all have the handouts we emailed you, right?**
- **You all have the meeting materials we sent you (by email), right?**

　配布資料　handout/handouts

　資料　material/materials

　全員に資料を配布する
　pass the handouts to everybody

　あらかじめ配布された資料を会議に持参する
　bring distributed handouts/materials to the meeting

▶ **本日のアジェンダをご覧ください。**

- **Please look at the agenda for today's meeting.**

▶ **本日の議題は次の通りです。**

- **Here's today's agenda.**
- **This is today's agenda.**

▶ 本日の議題の概要を説明します。
- Let me outline today's agenda.
- Let me go over today's agenda.

▶ すでにお知らせしたように、議題は3件です。
- As already mentioned, there are three items on the agenda.

すでにお知らせしたように（フォーマルな言い方）
as already informed, as already notified

前に触れたように（ソフトな言い方）
as previously mentioned, as I mentioned earlier,
as I touched on previously

さきほど話したとおり（もっともフレンドリー）
as I said earlier

"notified" は最もフォーマルな堅い表現で、政府機関からの正式な通達などに使われることが多く、"informed" もフォーマルです。それに比べて、"mentioned" は社内関係者間のやり取りなどによく使われ、"said" は最もフレンドリーです。

■会議の目的・概要

▶ 本日の会議の目的を説明させていただきます。
- Let me outline the purpose of today's meeting.

▶ 本会議の概要を簡単に説明します。
- Let me give you a brief overview of the meeting.

▶ 本日の会議の目的を明確にさせていただきます。
- I would like to clarify the purpose of today's meeting.
- Let me clarify the purpose of today's meeting.

▶ ご存知のように、この会議の目的は [A] です。
- As you all know, the purpose of this meeting is to [A].

［A］に入れる言葉の例：

新製品についてお知らせすること
inform you about our new products

新製品のマーケティングプランを立てること
make a marketing plan for our new product

今後のプロジェクトの進め方を明確にすること

make clear how we should proceed with the project
going forward

clarify how the project should proceed from here on

売上を向上させる方法について話し合うこと
discuss how to improve our sales

新商品の効果的な発売方法について話し合うこと
discuss how to effectively launch our new products

市場分析結果についてお知らせし、今後必要な対策について議論すること
inform you about the findings/results of our market
analysis and discuss necessary measures for the
future

顧客とのより緊密な関係を構築する方法について話し合うこと

discuss how to build closer relationships with our
customers

情報技術部全員で意見を交換すること
exchange opinions from all employees in the IT
department

計画実行のためのロードマップを作成すること
create a roadmap to implement our plan

■取り上げるトピックについて

▶ 今日は [B] について話し合いたいと思います。
- Today we're discussing [B].
- Today we'd like to discuss [B].
- We are here today to discuss [B].
- What we'd like to talk about today is [B].

[B] に入れる言葉の例：

新しい販売計画	our new sales plan
どのようにして売り上げを伸ばすか	how we can increase our sales
仕事の効率を向上させる方法	how to improve work efficiency
ウェブサイトの更新	updating our website
お得意様を惹きつける方法	how to attract customers/clients
新規顧客の獲得法	how to get new customers
顧客との信頼関係を築く方法	how we can build trust with clients

▶ 3つのトピックを取り上げる予定です。
- We're going to cover three topics/issues.

▶ アジェンダの最初の項目から始めましょう。
- Let's start with the first item on the agenda.

②個々のプレゼンテーション（各発表者から）

■挨拶・発表の場を与えてくれたことに感謝

▶ まず初めに、このような場を与えてくださりありがとうございます。

- Let me begin by saying that I appreciate the opportunity to appear here today.

▶ 今日は皆さんとお話しできてとても嬉しいです。

- I'm delighted to be speaking with you today.

▶ 本日、〜についてお話しできることを嬉しく思います。

- I'm delighted to be here today to tell you about 〜.

■自己紹介

▶ ごく手短に自己紹介させていただきます。

- I'll just briefly introduce myself.
- Let me quickly introduce myself.

▶ 私はR&D（研究開発部）で製品および市場調査を担当しております鈴木一郎です。

- I'm Ichiro Suzuki from the R&D department, responsible for product and market research.

▶ 私は山本浩二と申します。経営企画部長として、1ヵ月前に日本より赴任いたしました。

- I'm Koji Yamamoto. I was transferred here from Japan a month ago as head of the Corporate Planning Department.

▶ まず最初にお伝えさせていただきたいのですが、[C]。

• I would like to start by saying that [C].

[C] に入れる言葉の例：

> このプロジェクトのメンバーに選ばれたことを光栄に思います。
> it's a honor that I've been selected as a member of this project.
> it's a great honor for me to have been selected for this project.

> このプロジェクトのメンバーとして一緒に仕事ができることを楽しみにしています。
> I very much look forward to working together as a member of this project.

■テーマ・提案内容を伝える

▶ 今日は～についてお話させていただきます。

• Today I'm going to talk about ～
• I'd like to talk about ～

▶ 私の提案の概要をお話しします。

• I will briefly outline my proposal.

▶ 本日は次のようなご提案をさせていただきます：

• What I propose today is the following:
• I'd like to propose today the following:
• My proposal today is as follows:

▶ まず、今日このテーマを選んだ理由についてお話させて
いただきます。

• First, I'd like to talk about the reason why I chose
this topic today.

▶ こちらが私の計画案です。まずは要点をご説明させてい
ただきます。

• Here/This is the draft of my plan. First, let me
explain the main points.

▶ 手短に ～ の背景情報をお伝えさせていただきます。

• I'd like to briefly give you some background
information about ～ .

▶ メールに添付されていた資料をご覧ください。

• Please see the document attached to the email.

• Please take a look at the document attached to
the meeting invite.

▶ 我々の事業を持続可能なものへ変えるために私たちにで
きることは何か、概要をお伝えできればと思っています。

• I hope my presentation can give an overview on
what we can do to change our business into a
sustainable one.

概要　overview

全体像　whole picture, overall picture, big picture

■発表内容の構成

▶ 今日は３つのトピックに焦点を当てたいと思います。

• I am going to focus on three topics today.

▶ 3つの項目に分けてお話ししたいと思います。

- I have divided my presentation into 3 parts/ sections.
- My presentation is divided into 3 parts.

■発表資料の入手法

▶ 発表スライドはウェブサイトからダウンロードできますので、メモを取る必要はありません。

- You don't have to worry about taking notes, as the slides can be downloaded from our/the website.

▶ 会議後に発表スライドをメールでお送りします。

- I'll email the slides to everyone after the meeting.

■～をたたき台として議論する

▶ 私の考えをお伝えさせていただき、こちらを議論のたたき台としてご利用いただければと思います。

- I'll share some ideas, which I hope can be used as a basis for discussion.

たたき台（下書き）	a rough draft
たたき台を作成する	make a rough draft
たたき台を用意する	prepare a rough draft (of ～)
たたき台として使う	use as a basis for discussion
企画書／契約書の草案	a draft of the proposal/contract

例：話し合いのため契約書の草案を用意する
　　prepare a draft of the contract for discussion

■お役に立てれば幸い

▶ 〜 に関する基本的な知識を得ていただければ幸いです。

- I hope this presentation can provide you with some basic knowledge/information about 〜.

▶ 私の話が皆様のお役に立てれば幸いです。

- I hope my presentation will prove useful to/for * you.
- I hope my presentation will be helpful to everyone.
- I hope you will find this presentation useful.

---

* useful to you vs useful for you　"to" の場合は「特定の人」を対象にしており、"for" の場合は対象が「より広義で、より一般的」なニュアンスをもちます。

■休憩をはさむ・休憩後に具体的な計画を立てる

▶ ちょうど休憩の時間ですね。

- It's time for a break.

▶ 少し休憩しましょう。

- Let's take a short break.

▶ ここで少し休憩して、そのあとで具体的な計画を立てていきたいと思います。

- After taking a short break, I hope we can come up with a concrete plan.
- Let's take a short break here, after which I hope we can come up with a specific plan.

③討論内容に関する具体的な例

■〜について話す

▶ まずは、効果的な広告戦略について話します。

- We'll start/begin with discussing strategies for effective advertising.
- First, let's talk about effective advertising strategies.

まず初めに　First, Initially, To start with

次に　Second, After that, Then, Next

最後に　Finally, Lastly

討論内容の例

新製品開発の現状の確認	confirming the current status of new product development
ターゲットとする顧客層の特定	identifying a target audience
現在の広告手法の評価	evaluating current advertising methods
ソーシャルメディアの運用管理費も含めたコスト分析	conducting a cost analysis including social media operation and management costs
様々な広告手法のメリット・デメリット	discussing pros and cons of various advertising methods (advantages and disadvantages of 〜)
売上目標とコスト限度額の設定	setting sales targets and cost limits
タイムリーに広告を出す方法	discussing how to timely place ads

▶ 医療分野における人工知能（AI）技術の最新動向に焦点を
当ててお話ししたいと思います。

- I would like to focus on the latest trends of artificial
intelligence (AI) technology in the medical field.

▶ すでにお知らせしているように、今日は米国市場での当
社の認知度を高めるために何ができるかを話し合います。

- As already informed, today I will discuss what
we can do to increase the awareness of our
company in the US market.

▶ 本日の議題は、現在話題を集めている生成 AI についてです。

- Today's agenda is about Generative AI, which is
currently attracting attention.

生成 AI は、テキストや画像、音楽など、何か新しいものをつくる能力を持った人工知能（AI）
の一種。人間と同じような創造性を模倣し、新規の内容を自ら生み出す技術（NTT DATA よ
り一部を引用）。

■案・意見・アイデアを聞きたい

▶ 今日は売上の最大化について、皆さんの案を出していた
だきたいと思います。

- Today, I'd like you all to come up with your own
ideas on how to maximize sales.

▶ 我々の新技術について、どうやって新たな分野で宣伝す
れば効果的か、皆さんの意見を聞きたいと思います。

- I would like to hear your opinions on how we
can effectively advertise/promote our new
technology in these new areas.

▶ 当社は〜の分野ですでに世界的に知られていますが、全く異なる分野で新ブランドを確立するためにどうすればよいか、アイデアを出してほしいと思います。

• Our company is already known worldwide in the field of 〜 , so I would like you to come up with ideas on how we can establish a new brand in a completely different field.

■〜について議論したい

▶ 今日は、最も成功したリブランディングの例について議論したいと思います。

• Today we're discussing the most successful examples of rebranding.

• Today, I'd like to discuss some of the most successful rebranding examples.

▶ マーケティング戦略の効率化について議論したいと思います。

• I'd like to discuss with you how to improve the efficiency of our marketing strategy.

▶ 今日の会議では、新製品の発売に合わせて、メディアへの露出を最大限に高めるための、ソーシャルメディアマーケティング戦略について議論したいと思います。

• In today's meeting, I would like to discuss social media marketing strategies and how to get maximum media exposure for our new product launch.

ソーシャルメディアマーケティング (social media marketing) とは、X (Twitter), Facebook, Youtube, Instagram などのソーシャルメディアを、企業が活用して行うマーケティング戦略。

▶ 今日は、家庭用品からペットフードまで、購買決定権を握っている「お母さん達」を引きつける方法について議論したいと思います。

• Today we're discussing how to attract Moms, who make the purchasing decisions for almost everything, from household products to pet foods.

▶ ご存知のように、私たちは全く新しい事業分野への参入を目指して奮闘しているところです。

• As you all know, we have been struggling to enter a completely new field of business.

▶ 私たちの未来は、この新しい試みにかかっています。

• Our future depends on this new endeavor.

▶ 他社の成功例についてすでに資料をお渡ししていますが、それらはあくまでもヒントに過ぎません。わが社では全く異なる成功法を模索したいのです。

• I have already given you some material on the success stories of other companies, but they are just hints. We want to find a way to succeed in a completely different manner.

• Although we have already provided other companies' success stories, these are only hints. We want to find ways to succeed that are completely different/new.

④現状の問題と解決策について

■現状～のような問題がある

▶ 次に、現状の問題に移りたいと思います。
- Next, let's move on to the current problems/issues.

▶ 現状、～のような問題があります。
- Currently, there are problems like/such as ～:
- Currently, we have the following problems:

▶ 現状、我々はセキュリティ対策に問題があります。
- Currently, we have a problem with security measures.

▶ これが現在抱えている課題の一覧です：
- Here's a list of the challenges/issues/problems we currently have:

課題の例　issues, challenges, problems

品質改善	quality improvement
開発工程の効率化	how to improve the efficiency of the development process
広告方法	how to advertise, the advertising method
製品の導入法	how to introduce our products
AI（人工知能）を活用したサービス	services using AI, AI-powered services
経費削減法	cost reduction methods
認知度向上法	methods to raise awareness

▶ ～ についてもう少し詳しく説明いたします。

• Let me give you some more information on/ regarding ～ .

■問題の解決策について

▶ この問題の解決策として、私は～の情報を探し始めました。

• In order to solve this problem, I started looking for information on/about ～

▶ この問題を解決するには、まず最初に、米国市場での当社の認知度を高める必要があると思いました。

• To address this issue, I thought it's first necessary to increase our company awareness in the US market.

この問題に対処するために　　to address this issue
これを解決するために　　　　in order to solve this problem

▶ この問題は [D] でしか解決できないと思います。

• This problem can only be solved by [D].

[D] に入れる言葉の例：

リスクを明確化すること	clarifying the risks
現システムから新システムへの移行	replacing the current system with a new one
詳細な市場分析	a detailed market analysis
新方式を使うこと	using a new method
試行錯誤の繰り返し	trial and error

⑤スライド・図・データで説明

■スライドや図を提示して説明

▶ このスライドは重要なポイントを示したものです。

- **This slide shows the key points.**

▶ このスライド／図／円グラフは [E] を示したものです。

- **This slide/graph/pie chart shows [E].**

   示す、説明する、例証（実証）する、レビューする、要約する、図解する、描写（表現）する

   show, describe, demonstrate, review, summarize, Illustrate, depict

[E] に入れる言葉の例：

新旧製品の違い	the differences between our old and new products
既存製品の改良点	the improvements to our existing products
既存製品へ新たに追加された付加価値	the newly added value to our existing products
市場調査の結果	the results of the market research
今回実施した市場調査の方法	how the market research was conducted this time

■〜をもとに作成した資料

▶ 本資料は7月31日現在の情報をもとに作成したものです。

- **This document was made/created based on information/data as of July 31.**

▶ これは最新の統計データをもとに、今日の会議用に作成した資料です。

• These are the materials I prepared for today's meeting, based on the latest statistics.

■〜の目的で作成した素案

▶ これは次にウェブサイトを更新するための素案です。

• Here's the draft of what will be included in the next website update.

▶ これは皆様からコメントや提案を募るために作成した素案です。

• This is a draft prepared for the purpose of inviting comments and suggestions from you.

▶ これは皆さんにレビューおよびフィードバックしていただくための素案です。

• Here's the draft I need everyone to review and give feedback on.

■円グラフ

▶ この円グラフは、自宅でコンピュータを使用する人の年齢分布を示しています。

• This pie chart shows the age distribution of/for those who use computers at home.

▶ 円グラフは視覚的に理解しやすく、比率を強調するのに便利です．

• Pie charts are easy to visually understand and are useful for emphasizing/highlighting ratios.

■棒グラフ

▶ この棒グラフは、我々のプロジェクトに関わる費用の内訳を示しています。

• This bar graph shows the cost breakdown of/for our project.

内訳　breakdown, details, detailed breakdown

▶ この棒グラフは、パンデミックによるロックダウン以降、急激に売上が減少したことを示しています。

• This bar graph shows a sudden drop in sales since the lock-down due to the pandemic.

■横軸と縦軸・線の種類・線の色について説明

▶ 横軸は時間、縦軸は M サイズを着る人数を表しています。

• The X (horizontal) axis represents time, and the Y (vertical) axis represents the number of people wearing medium size.

▶ ご覧のように、この図の赤い部分が〜を示しています。

• As you can see, the red part of this graph shows 〜 .

▶ 破線は〜を、実線は〜を、曲線は〜を示しています。

• The broken line represents 〜 , the solid line shows 〜 , and the curved line describes 〜 .

▶ 緑色の線は〜を、淡い緑色の線は〜を示しています。

• The green line indicates 〜 , and the pale green line indicates 〜 .

円グラフ	pie chart / pie graph
折れ線グラフ	line chart / line graph
棒グラフ	bar chart / bar graph
ヒストグラム	histogram
フローチャート	flow chart
表	table
図	figure / chart / diagram
写真	picture
横軸	X (horizontal) axis
縦軸	Y (vertical) axis
実線	solid line
点線	dotted line
破線	dashed line
曲線	curved line
分布	distribution
網掛けの部分	shaded area
斜線の部分	hatched/shaded area
表の上部	at the top of the table
表の中央部	in the middle of the table
表の下部	at the bottom of the table

■増加・減少を％で示す

▶ 我々の目標は少なくとも売上の 15% アップ、利益の 10% アップです。

• Our goal is to increase sales and profits by at least 15 and 10 percent respectively.

▶ どうすれば売上 10%増を達成できるか、いくつかの案（戦略）を考えてみました。

• I have come up with some ideas/strategies on how to achieve a 10% increase in sales.

▶ 売上を 20%増大させるためのいくつかの方法をご紹介します。

• I'll share with you several ways to increase sales by 20%.

• Here are some ways/ideas to boost sales by 20%.

▶ 昨年はパンデミックで不要不急のビジネスがすべて閉鎖されたため、売上が 70%減少しました。

• Sales fell by 70% last year as the pandemic shut down all non-essential businesses.

• Sales dropped by 70% last year as all non-essential businesses were closed due to the pandemic .

non-essential 必須ではない、本質的ではない

non-urgent 緊急ではない、急を要さない

▶ 為替レートの不利な変動により、前年同期に比べて大幅な売上減となりました。

• There was a substantial drop in sales compared to the same time/period last year due to unfavorable fluctuations in exchange rates.

⑥四捨五入・切り上げ・切り下げ

四捨五入	rounding, rounding off
切り上げる／切り下げる	round up/round down
小数点	decimal point
小数点以下	after the decimal point
整数	whole number, integer

■四捨五入

▶ 小数点以下は四捨五入してください。

- Round decimals to the nearest whole number.
- Round off the decimals.

▶ 四捨五入して整数にしてください（整数に丸める）。

- Please round (off) to the nearest integer/whole number.

▶ 10円未満は四捨五入してください。

- Please round off amounts less than 10 yen.
- Please round (off) to the nearest 10 yen.

これは502円だったけど、500円くれればいいですよ。
This was 502 yen, but you can give me 500 yen.
This was 502 yen, but you can round to 500 yen.

■切り上げ・切り下げ

▶ 小数点以下は切り上げてください。
- Please round up to the nearest whole number.

▶ 小数点以下は切り下げてください。
- Please round down to the nearest whole number.
- Please ignore numbers below the decimal point.

Coffee Break
── 愚痴を聞いてくれる？

vent （溜まっていた不満や怒りなどの）はけ口（名）、
　　　　発散する（動）
rant （抑えきれない怒りを周囲にわめく）わめき（名）、
　　　　どなり散らす（動）

電話してごめんね、愚痴らせて！
- Sorry for calling, I just need to vent!

愚痴りたくなったら私に電話してね。
- Call me if you need to vent.

誰かに愚痴を聞いてほしい（愚痴を言える相手が必要）。
- I need someone to vent to.

ちょっと時間ある？ 愚痴りたいんだけど。
- Do you have a minute？　I need to vent.

いいよ。聞いてあげるよ。
- Go ahead.　I'm all ears.

愚痴っちゃってごめんね。
- Sorry I needed/had to vent.
- Sorry for venting like this.
（溜まっていた不平不満を漏らしたあとに言う）

⑦提案する・見解を述べる

■提案する

▶ 〜について提案があります

- I'd like to make a proposal for 〜
- I'd like to make a suggestion about how to 〜
- I'd like to suggest that we 〜

▶ どうすれば売上を上げられるか、考えがあります。

- I have an idea on how to increase our sales.

  私の提案（考え）は〜
  My suggestion is 〜
  My thoughts are 〜
  I'd (I would) say that 〜

▶ 〜について私のアイデアを提案したいです。

- I'd like to pitch/propose my idea about 〜

  pitch：アイデアを売り込む、自分の考えが良いと思うので売り込みたい

■見解を述べる

▶ これについてはじっくり考えてみました。

- I've given this a lot of thought/consideration.

  〜について熟考する、思案する
  give a lot of thought to 〜
  give 〜 a lot of thought
  put a lot of thought into 〜
  spend a lot of (time and) thought on 〜

  〜について多くの時間と労力を費やす
  take a lot of time and effort to 〜

▶ あくまでも私の意見ですが〜

- **It's just my opinion, but/however 〜**

  あくまでも私の考えですが〜
  In my opinion, 〜
  （メール文などでは IMO と省略）

  僭越ながら私見ではありますが〜
  In my humble opinion, 〜
  （メール文などでは IMHO と省略）

  いろいろ検討した上での考えですが（熟考した考えですが）、
  After much consideration, 〜
  In my considered opinion, 〜
  （メール文などでは IMCO と省略）

▶ 私の経験では〜

- **In my experience, 〜**

▶ 個人的な見解ですが〜（私に言わせれば〜）

- **From my (personal) perspective, 〜**
- **From my (personal) point of view, 〜**
- **This is (just) my personal opinion, but 〜**

▶ あくまでも個人的な見解ですが、多くの人はマスコミの
報道を鵜呑みにしていると思います。

- **This is just my personal opinion, but I feel that
  many people simply trust what is reported in
  the media.**

- **It's only my personal viewpoint, but I feel that
  many people simply accept media reports at
  face value.**

  〜を額面通りに受け取る
  take/accept 〜 at face value

⑧〜であることは明らか・自明の理

■〜が明らかである

▶ 〜であることは明らかです。
- It's clear/obvious that 〜 .

▶ この図から〜が明白です
- (As you can see) from this graph, it's clear that 〜
- It's quite obvious/evident from this diagram that 〜

  この図から、世界が恐ろしいパンデミックを経験していることは明らかです。

  It is quite obvious from this graph that the world is experiencing a terrible pandemic.

▶ このグラフからまずわかることは〜
- The first thing you can see from this graph is 〜 .

▶ 〜ということが（ますます）明らかになりつつあります。
- It's becoming more (and more) obvious that 〜 .
- It's becoming (increasingly) evident that 〜 .

■説明する必要がないほど明らか

▶ 自明の理です。
- It's self-evident.
- It's obvious.

▶ 事実は一目瞭然です（説明不要です）。
- The fact is self-explanatory.
- The fact is so clear/evident that it does not require explanation.

▶ この目標達成のためには、もっと予算が必要なのは明らかです。

- It's clear/obvious that we need more budget to hit these targets.

■〜は言うまでもない・〜は言うに及ばず

▶ もちろん、勉強すればするほど英語が上達するのは言うまでもありません。

- Of course, it goes without saying that the more you study the better your English will be.

【文頭にくることが多い（必ずではない）】

It goes without saying 〜
Needless to say 〜

【文の途中、もしくは最後にくることが多い】

not to mention
to say nothing of 〜, let alone 〜

彼は疲れ切っていて、走ることはおろか歩くことさえ出来なかった。
He was too tired to walk, let alone run.

私は英語を書くことはおろか、話すことさえできない。
I can't speak English, let alone write it.

▶ この方法が最善の解決策かどうかはわかりませんが、共通の価値観に基づく経営理念の確立が重要であることは言うまでもありません。

- I'm not sure if this is the best solution, however, it goes without saying that it is important to establish a management philosophy centered/rooted in shared values.

この方法が最良の解決策であるかどうかは明らかではありませんが、〜
I'm not sure if this is the best solution, but 〜
Whether this method is the best solution is unclear, but 〜

▶ 言うまでもなく、[F] を確立することが最重要です。

● Needless to say, it is most important to establish [F].

[F] に入れる言葉の例

再発防止策	measures to prevent it from happening again
人材育成のシステム	a system to develop human resources
効果的な研修システム	an effective training system
強力なサイバーセキュリティ戦略	strong cybersecurity strategies
役立つ情報を提供するシステム	a system to provide useful information
共通の価値観に根ざした経営理念	a management philosophy rooted in shared values
独自のアイデンティティと製品の差別化	a unique identity and product differentiation
定期的会合によりチームメンバーの共通認識	a common/shared understanding among team members through regular meetings
充実した人員体制	a well-staffed organizational structure

⑨説明を求める

■何を言いたいのかわからない

▶ 申し訳ありませんが、何を言いたいのかわかりません。
- I'm sorry but I don't get your point.
- I'm sorry to say but I don't get what you mean.
- I don't see what you're getting at.

▶ ○○○とはどういう意味ですか？
- What do you mean by ○○○?

▶ すみませんが、あなたが何を言いたいのか、あまり明確にわかりません。
- I'm having trouble understanding what you mean.
- Sorry, but I'm not clear about what you mean.

■もう少し詳しく・具体的に説明してほしい

▶ もう少し詳しく説明していただけますか？
- Could you (please) explain it in more detail?
- Could you explain it in a little more detail?
- Could you elaborate a bit more?
- Could you expand on that?

44

▶ もう少し具体的に教えていただけますか？

● **Please be more specific.**

もう少し詳しく
〜 in a little more detail
〜 a bit more about 〜

もう少し具体的に
a bit more specific (about) 〜

▶ 今おっしゃったことについて、もう少し詳しくお聞かせ
いただけますか？

● **Could you elaborate a bit more on what you just said?**

▶ この問題に関するお考えについて詳しく説明してくださ
いますか？

● **Could you elaborate on your thoughts regarding this issue?**

■正確（具体的）に説明してほしい

▶ それが何を意味するのか正確に話していただけますか？

● **Could/Can you please tell us exactly what you mean by that?**

▶「システムを再起動する」とは、具体的には何を意味する
のでしょうか？

● **What exactly do you mean by "reboot the system"?**

■背景情報について説明していただきたい

▶ 〜について、もう少し背景を説明していただけますか？

- **Can you please give us (some) more background 〜**
  あなたの考え／あなたが考えていること
  〜 regarding your idea?
  〜 on what you are thinking?

▶ 何をしようとしているのか、その背景をもう少し教えて
  いただけますか？

- **Can you please give us some more background information on what you're trying to do?**

- **Could you tell us a little more about the background of what you are up to?**

Coffee Break
― 既成概念にとらわれずに

think outside the box
not be confined by conventional thinking
not to get caught up with conventional thinking
think freely

既成概念にとらわれずに考えてくださいね

- Please think freely, and not get caught up
  with conventional thinking.

- I want you all to start thinking outside the box.

⑩質問を受ける・意見を促す

■質問・意見はありますか？

▶ ご質問はありませんか？
- Do you have any questions?
- Are there any questions?

▶ 意見（考え）を聞かせてもらえませんか？
- Can you please tell me your opinion?
- I'd like to hear your opinion.
- What do you think?
- What are your thoughts?

▶ それについて何か意見（考え）はありますか？
- May I have your comments on this?
- Could I have your thoughts on this?
- Any comments?

■意見を促す

▶ ご意見（見解）をお聞きしたいです。
- I'd like to have/hear your opinion.
- I'd like to have/hear your point of view.
- I'd like to have/hear your views on ～ .

▶ ～について、山田さんのお考えをお聞きしたいです。
- I'd like to ask Mr. Yamada for his view/thoughts on ～ .
- Can I hear what Mr. Yamada has to say about ～?

▶ 山田さんもこちらの意見に賛同か知りたいです。
- I'd like to know if Mr. Yamada shares this opinion.
- Mr. Yamada, do you agree with this opinion?

▶ （どうしたら改善できるか）あなたの考えをお聞きしたいです。
- I would love to hear your thoughts (on how we can make any improvements).

▶ これについてどう思いますか？
- What do you think about this?
- How do you feel about this?
- Do you have anything to say about that?

■コメントを促す

▶ 他に何か提案（コメント）はありますか？
- Do you have any other suggestions?
- Any other comments?

■追加したいことは？

▶ 他に追加することはありますか？
- Do you have anything to add?
- Is there anything you'd like to add?

■前向きな意見・どんな意見でも歓迎

▶ 問題点よりも、解決策に焦点を当てて、前向きなフィードバックをお願いします。

- Please keep your feedback positive, focusing more on the solution and less on the problem.

▶ より良い、より持続可能な未来の実現のため、皆さんのアイデアをお聞かせください。

- Please share your ideas to achieve a better and more sustainable future.

▶ ユニークな案や奇抜な案でも歓迎します。

- Unique or even eccentric ideas are welcome.

  奇抜な wacky, 斬新な novel
  型破りな（型にはまらない）unconventional
  独自の unusual, ユニークな unique

Coffee Break
― 時間の問題

just/only a matter of time

人工知能が人類の知能を超えるのは
もはや時間の問題に過ぎない。

- It's now only a matter of time before AI (artificial intelligence) surpasses human intelligence.

⑪長所と短所を評価する

■長所と短所

advantage(s) and disadvantage(s)

賛否（両論）、長所と短所 pros and cons

本社移転の是非
pros and cons of relocating the head office

リモートワークの是非
pros and cons of remote working

賛成論と反対論（長所と短所）のリスト
list of pros and cons

長所と短所、強みと弱み
strengths and weaknesses
strong points and weak points

▶ 長所は〜、短所は〜です。
- **The advantage is 〜, the disadvantage is 〜.**
- **The advantages are 〜, the disadvantages are 〜.**

■利点と欠点の両方を考慮

▶ 利点と欠点の両方を評価しなければなりません。
- **We have to assess both the advantages and disadvantages.**

評価する evaluate、考慮する consider、議論する discuss

▶ プラス面だけでなくマイナス面の影響も考慮して決断をくだす必要があります。
- **We have to make our decision by taking into consideration the positive as well as the negative effects.**

▶ そうすることで、私達はより自信を持ってその問題に取り組むことができます。

- By doing this, we can be more confident in tackling the issue.

▶ その方法は個人的な偏見や感情に影響されにくいです。

- The method is less likely to be influenced by personal biases and emotions.

■長所と短所の一覧を作成

▶ グループで意思決定を行うための最も効果的な方法のひとつは、長所と短所（プロコン）リストの作成です。

- One of the most effective ways to make a group decision is to create a list of pros and cons.

▶ メリットとデメリットを書き出すと、意志決定プロセスにおいてより客観的な判断ができます。

- Writing down the advantages and disadvantages makes the decision making process less subjective.

▶ 長所と短所を列挙することは、目の前の問題をよりよく分析するのに役立ちます。
最終的な決断を下す際の心構えができます。

- To list pros and cons can help us better analyze the issue at hand.
It will make us more prepared when making our final decision.

▶ 長所と短所の一覧を作成するのは非常に簡単です。

- Making a list of pros and cons is very easy.

▶ 長所と短所の一覧があれば、中立的でより客観的な人に
  レビューしてもらうことができます。

- With a list of pros and cons, we can have our
  decision reviewed by someone neutral and
  more objective.

■一長一短がある

▶ この方法は（〜に関して）、一長一短があります。

- This method has both advantages and
  disadvantages (in terms of 〜).

▶ それぞれの考え方には一長一短があります。

- Each of these ideas has its own merits and demerits.

Coffee Break
― 責任を転嫁する

shift the blame/responsibility (onto others)
put the blame on someone else

自分のミスを他人に転嫁するのは良くないです。

- It's not good to shift the blame onto others for
  your own mistakes.

"onto"を使うべきか"on to"を使うべきかを見分ける方法：
ontoはonとuponの同義語なので、uponで入れ替えOKならば
ontoが正解です。
She put it onto the table = She put it upon the table.

下記は"on to"としなければならない例です。
短い休憩後、その歌手はステージに戻り、次の曲を歌い続けた。
After a brief break, the singer walked back <u>onto</u> the
stage and continued <u>on to</u> her next song.

⑫同意する・賛成する

■同感・全面的に賛成・考えを支持

▶ あなたの意見に賛成です。

- **I agree with you.**

  人と意見が一致する agree with someone
  その点はあなたと同意見です。
  I agree with you on that.

▶ 私もすべての点で同意見です。

- **I agree with you in every respect.**
- **I completely agree with you.**

▶ 私もほとんどの点で同意見です。

- **I agree with you on most points.**

▶ その提案に賛成です。

- **I'm in favor of the proposal.**

▶ あなたの考えを支持します。

- **I (can) support your idea.**

▶ あなたのおっしゃっていることを全面的に支援します。

- **I fully support what you're saying.**

  全面的に　fully, completely
  無条件で　without reservation, unconditionally
  ほぼ、おおかたは　mostly (but 〜 が続くことが多い)
  ほぼ同意しますが、問題はコストなのです。
  I mostly agree (with you), but the problem is the cost.

▶ あなたの考えに共感します。
- I share your opinion/thoughts.

▶ その通りだと思います。
- I think you're right.

▶ それは良いアイデアだと思います。
- I think that's a good idea.

▶ そうするべきだと思います。
- I think we should do that.

▶ いいと思います。
- **That sounds good.**

▶ 私も同じように考えています。
- **I feel the same way.**

▶ 私も同じ考えです。
- **I'm on the same page.**

   考えを共有している、（複数の人が）同じ考えである、共通の情
   報や認識を持っている
   be on the same page

   我々みんな同じ考え（認識）でしょうか？
   Are we all on the same page?

   このプロジェクトを進める前に、全員が共通の認識を持ってい
   なければならない。
   We need to get everyone on the same page before we
   can move forward with this project.

"on the same page" については p104 を参照

▶ 私も同感（賛成）です。

- I second that.
- I share your opinion.

    A 氏「これが最高だ」
    ➡ B 氏「同感（賛成）です」
    Mr. A "This is the best."
    ➡ Mr. B "I second that.", "I share your opinion"

■理にかなっている

▶ 理にかなっています（それなら納得がいきます）。

- That makes sense.

▶ それは理にかなっているように思えます（もっともだと思います）。

- That sounds reasonable (to me).

■ある程度・部分的に・原則的に賛成

    ある程度、部分的に賛成
    to some extent, to a certain extent, to an extent
    ある点までは　up to a point
    部分的に　partly (agree to your idea)

▶ 原則的には賛成ですが、実際にそうなるかは疑問です。

- I agree in principle, but I doubt if it will happen in practice.

    原則的には（おおむね、大筋では）
    in principle, (but 〜を伴うことが多い)

▶ ある程度は賛成なのですが、状況はおそらくもっと複雑でしょうね。

• I agree with you to an extent, but surely the situation is more complex than that.

▶ あなたに同意するつもりです。

• I'm inclined to agree with you.

be inclined to 〜　〜したいと思う、（気持ちが）傾いている。

■賛成だが、細部の詰めが必要

▶ 主な点については賛成ですが、細部についてはもっと詰めが必要と思います。

• I agree with you on the main points, but I think you need to elaborate on the details.

• I agree with the main points, but I think more details should be worked out.

細部の詰めが必要
details need to be worked out

詰めが甘い
not thorough enough, not detailed and careful enough

細部の詰めが甘かったと思います。
I think the details were not carefully worked out/ considered.

細部を詰めましょう。
Let's finalize the details.
Let's nail down the details.

"nail" は「釘を打つ」意味ですが、"nail down" は「確定する、確認する、決定する」などの意味があります。

➡ Coffee Break "完璧にできたね！ You nailed it!"（p89）を参照

⑬同意できない・どちらかというと反対・ソフトに反対

同意できない
be opposed to (something) /be against
can't agree
can't accept
can't go along with (someone, something)

（計画、提案などに）賛同できません。
I can't go along with (the plan, suggestion, someone's request).

■賛成か反対か意見を聞く

▶ この問題について、どのようなスタンスをお持ちですか？

- **What's your stance on this issue?**

▶ あなたは賛成ですか、反対ですか？

- **Do you agree or disagree?**
- **Are you for or against it?**

  我々の提案に賛成ですか、反対ですか？
  Are you for or against our proposal?

  支持者と反対者
  supporters and opponents

  "proponents"（支持者）は "opponents" の対となる言葉ですが、実際にはあまり使われていないようです。

▶ あなたはこの案に賛成ですか？

- **Are you in favor of this proposal?**
- **Do you agree with this proposal?**

▶ 本社の移転に反対ですか？

- **Are you opposed to the head office relocation?**
- **Are you against relocating the head office?**

■同意できない

▶ 恐縮ですが、あなたの（〜）に同意できません。
- I'm sorry, but I don't/can't agree with you (about 〜).

▶ 申し訳ないですが、その企画に賛同できません
- I'm afraid to say, but I can't agree with that plan.

▶ その件について、私は（田中さんに）同意できません。
- I can't agree (with Mr. Tanaka) on that matter.

■あまり同意できない・どちらかというと反対（ソフトな表現）

▶ どちらかというと反対です。
- I'm rather opposed to it.
- I'm rather against it.

▶ 全て賛成というわけではありません。（丁寧な部分否定）
- I don't quite agree.

▶ 私は同意しかねます。
- I'm inclined to disagree.

    どちらかというと、〜の傾向がある tend to 〜
    〜したいと思う、（気持ちが）傾いている　be inclined to 〜
    若い企業は古い企業よりも大胆で、かつリスクを取る傾向があると言えるかもしれません。
    One might say that younger companies tend to be bolder and more risk-taking than older companies.

■ソフトに反対する

▶ 正直に言うと、私はその案に反対です。
- **To be honest with you, I disagree with the idea.**

▶ あなたの意見を尊重しますが、その考えには反対です。
- **I respect your point, but I'm against the idea.**

▶ 言いたいことはわかりますが、しかし〜
- **I see/understand what you're saying, but, ...**

▶ それも一理ありますが、しかし〜
- **That's a good/fair point, but....**

▶ この点については同意しかねますが…
- **I'm not sure I agree with you on this point....**
  それはどうかと思います。
  I'm not sure about that.

▶ もし自分の意見を言ってもよければ、あなたの企画に賛同できません。
- **If I'm entitled to my opinion, I cannot agree with your plan.**
- **If you don't mind me giving my opinion, I don't agree with your plan.**

▶ 個人的な意見ですが、もう少し淡い色の方が良いように思います。
- **I personally think something a little paler would look better.**

▶ しかしながら、すでに似たような商品で多くの在庫を抱えています。
- However, we already have a large inventory of similar products.

▶ 少し現実離れしているように思えます。
- That sounds a little bit too unrealistic to me.

■視点・見方・価値観が異なる

▶ 私は違う見方をしています。
- I see it differently.
- That's not how I see it.

▶ これが私の見方です。
- This is how I'm seeing it.

▶ 申し訳ありませんが、私は違う意見を持っています。
- I'm sorry to say, but I have a different opinion.

▶ 誰かの意見を批判するつもりはありません。
- I'm not going to criticize anyone's opinion.

▶ 私達はこの問題について異なる価値観と異なる視点を持っているようです。
- It seems we have different values and perspectives on this issue.

▶ 私たちはこの問題を別の視点から見ています。
- We're looking at this issue from different perspectives.

▶ あなたの意見を支持したいのですが、私はこの問題を
　別の視点から捉えています。

- I would like to support your view, but I see the
  issue from a different perspective.

▶ あなたの言い分はわかりますが、私はそうは思いません。

- I take your point, but that's not the way I see it.

  私が思うには、私の考えでは、私が見たところ〜
  The way I see it 〜

  私が思うには、まだ書き直す時間はあります。
  The way I see it, we still have time to rewrite it.

▶ もし反対だったり、別の見方があるというのなら、どう
　いう風に見ておられるのか説明してください。ぜひお聞
　きしたいです。

- If you disagree or have another perspective,
  just explain it the way you're seeing it. I'd be
  happy to listen to you.

Coffee Break ― ちょっと休憩

ここで少し休憩にしましょう。
- Let's take a short break here.
- Let's have a quick break.
- Shall we break for a few minutes?

午後3時までに戻ってください。
- Please come back by 3 pm.
- Please come back before 3 pm.

Coffee Break
― よくぞ言ってくれた！その通り！同感！いいね！

よくぞ言ってくれた！
- Well said!
- Well stated!

全く同感！その通り！
- I agree 100%
- I agree with you!
- You said it!

そうだ！その通り！
- You are so right!
- Exactly!
- That's right!

全くその通り！（それ以上に上手く言えない）
- Couldn't have said it better (myself)！

同感！まさにその通り！
- I'm with you!
- My point exactly!
  (= That's exactly my point!)

おっしゃることはわかります／全くですね／
ごもっともですね。（相手に理解や共感を示す）
- I hear what you're saying.

大賛成！
- I couldn't agree more!

賛成！（OKです！）いいね！
- I give you/it a thumbs up!

すごくいいね！最高！（両手の親指を立てて、「いいね」）
- Wow, two thumbs up!
- I give you/it two thumbs up!

もし先方が I don't think …… と否定形だった時に
賛同する場合：
- Me neither!
- Neither do I.
- I don't either.
- I don't think so too.
- I don't think so either.

【イギリスでよく使われる】
その通り！どんぴしゃ！
- Spot on!
- 100% spot on!
- That's spot on!
- You're spot on!
  （最近は米国でも使われています）

⑭強く反対する

■強く反対・全く賛成できない

disagree with (someone)、disagree to (something) だけでも強く反対するニュアンスですが、さらに強い反対を表現する場合は：

強く反対する strongly disagree with, strongly against

激しく反対・猛反対する
be vehemently against, vehemently oppose

▶ 申し訳ないですが、全く賛成できません。
- Sorry, I can't agree at all.
- I'm afraid but/that I have to disagree.

▶ その考えに強く反対します。
- I'm strongly against the idea.
- I'm strongly opposed to the idea.

▶ （あなたと）全く意見が合いません。
- I am in total disagreement (with you).

▶ 率直に言って、全く同意できません。
- To be honest, I strongly disagree with you.

▶ あなたのアイデアは全く受け入れられません。
- There is no way I can accept your idea.

⑮矛盾を指摘する

■矛盾している

▶ あなたの言っていることは矛盾しています。

- There's a contradiction in your explanation.
- There's a contradiction in what you're saying.
- There are several contradictions in your explanation.
- Your explanation is inconsistent.
- The explanation has many inconsistencies.

▶ その説明は今おっしゃったことと矛盾しています。

- That explanation goes against what was just said.

▶ その説明は他の情報と矛盾しています。

- That explanation is inconsistent with the other information.

　～と矛盾する　contradict

　矛盾した（形容詞）、相反している　be contradictory

　一貫性がない　be inconsistent (with) ～

　矛盾だらけ
　be full of contradictions
　be full of inconsistencies
　a bundle of contradictions

　このプランには矛盾がある。　There is a contradiction in this plan.

　人が～するのは矛盾している　It's contradictory for someone to ～

▶ おっしゃっていることが矛盾していると思いませんか？

- Don't you think you're contradicting yourself?
- Don't you think you're being inconsistent?

▶ あなたのアイデアは矛盾だらけと言わざるを得ません。

• I have to say that your idea is full of inconsistencies/
contradictions.

▶ リモートワークには柔軟性の向上、通勤時間の短縮、満
員電車に乗るストレスからの解放などのメリットがあり
ます。しかしその一方で、運動不足、社会的交流の減少、
仕事と私生活の境界があいまいになるなどの課題があり
ます。さらに、家庭で過ごす時間が増えた一方で、長時
間働き過ぎて家庭を犠牲にするというような矛盾も指摘
されています。

• Remote work has advantages such as increased
flexibility, shorter commuting time, and eliminating
the stress of riding on crowded trains. On the other
hand, however, there are disadvantages such as lack
of exercise, reduced social interaction, and blurring of
lines between work and personal life. Furthermore,
contradictions have been pointed out, such as spending
more time at home but actually working too many
hours and sacrificing family life.

Coffee Break
― 誤解しないでね

Don't get me wrong.

誤解しないでくださいね（変に取らないでね）。
ただあなたの意見が聞きたかっただけです。

• Please don't take this the wrong way.
  I just wanted your input (on this).

完全に誤解していますよ！（ひどい誤解ですよ！）

• You have it all wrong!
• You've got it all wrong!
• You have me all wrong!

⑯相反する

■相反する

▶ 彼のアイデアは私の考えと相反するものです。
- His idea conflicts with mine.
- His idea is incompatible with mine.
- His idea is at odds with mine.

▶ 我々の利益は彼らの利益と相反します。
- Our interests conflict (with theirs).
- Our interests are incompatible (with theirs).
- We have conflicting interests (with them).

▶ ソーシャルメディアで流れている相反する情報に混乱した人は少なくないでしょう。
- Many people have felt confused by conflicting information circulating on social media.

■相容れない・互換性がない

▶ そのような考えは私たちの考えとまったく相容れないものです。
- Such an idea is totally incompatible with ours.

▶ そのインクカートリッジはこのプリンターと互換性がありません。
- The ink cartridge is incompatible with this printer.

⑰比較できない

■比較のしようがない

▶ ～については、日本と米国では文化が違うので比較のしようがありません。

- Regarding ～ , there's no way to compare Japan and the US because their cultures are different.
- Regarding ～ , we can't compare Japan and the US as they have different cultures.

■リンゴとオレンジを比較しても意味がない

▶ 比べる土台が異なるので、比べようがない。
  （それはリンゴとオレンジを比べるようなものだ）

- It's (kind of) like comparing apples and/with/to oranges.（諺）
- You can't compare apples and oranges.

▶ リンゴとオレンジを比べても意味がない。

- There's no point comparing apples and oranges.

Coffee Break
― ちなみに補足すると

ちなみに補足すると as a side note (on a side note)
同義語：by the way, just for the record, incidentally,
　　　　as an aside など

余談ですが、先日当社の研究者と話をする機会がありました。

- Just as a side note, I recently had the chance to speak with one of our researchers.

⑱代替案を提案・検討を勧める

■代替案を提案

▶ 代替案を提案してもよろしいでしょうか？
- May I propose an alternative?
- Can I suggest an alternative plan?

代替案をいくつか提案したいです。
I'd like to propose some alternative plans.

▶ 提案してもよろしいですか？
- May (Can) I make a suggestion?

■検討を勧める

▶ 私の意見ですが、これらの記事を検討することをお勧めします。
- In my opinion, I would suggest you to review these articles.

▶ 私の意見としては、現在の価格の維持をお勧めします。値上げには反対です。
- If you ask me, I would recommend maintaining the current price. I'm against the price increase.

値上げ
price increase
raising the price
price hike

ここ1，2年の食料品やガソリンの値上げはひどいものです。
The price hikes for food and gas in the last year or two have been terrible.

■むしろ〜・〜よりむしろ

▶ 結論を急ぐ必要はないと思います。
むしろ、より深い議論をするためにもっと時間をかける
べきです。

• I think we don't have to rush to a conclusion.
Rather, we should take the extra time for
deeper discussion.

むしろ
rather

〜よりむしろ
rather than

代わりに（他の選択肢として）
instead, alternatively, as an alternative (to), as another option

▶ 当初の案に固執するより、むしろ他の選択肢を検討すべ
きと思います。

• Rather than sticking to the original plan, I think
we should consider other options.

▶ 人件費削減ありきで検討するよりもむしろ、まずは我々
の通常の業務を見直し、改善すべき点について議論すべ
きです。

• Rather than focusing on reducing labor costs, we
should first review our normal work and discuss
areas to improve.

▶ Ａ案よりも、むしろＢ案のほうが訴求効果が高いと思い
ます。

• I think plan B is rather more appealing than plan A.

⑲即答を避ける・検討する・考えさせてほしい

■即答を避ける

▶ 今即答するのは避けたいです。
- I'd like to avoid giving an immediate answer now.

▶ 申し訳ありませんが、すぐにはお答えできません。
- I'm afraid I can't give any immediate answer.

▶ 申し訳ありませんが、その件については現時点でどうお答えすればいいかわかりません。
- I'm afraid I really don't know what to say right now on that matter.

■検討する・検討が必要

▶ 検討させていただきます。
- I'll consider it.
- I'll take it into consideration.

▶ さらなる検討が必要です。
- Further consideration is needed.

▶ それはいい質問ですね、真剣に検討させていただきます。
- That's a good question. Let me give it some serious thought.

▶ あなたの質問に明確にお答えするには、さらなる作業（研究）が必要です。
- Further work is needed before a definitive answer can be given to your question.

■少し考えさせてほしい

▶ 少し考えてみます。
- Let me give it some thought.
- I'll give it some thought.

▶ これについては少し考えさせてください。
- I need more time to think about it.

▶ 調べるのに少し時間が必要です。
- I'll need some time to look into it.

▶ それはいいご指摘ですね。考えさせてください。
- That's a good point. Let me think about it.

▶ 少し考えてもいいですか？
- Can I sleep on it?
- Let me sleep on it (for a few days).

   ひと晩考えてみて判断する、少し時間を置いて考える
   sleep on = think more about something overnight and
   make a decision about it later.

   どうぞしばらく考えてから返事をください
   Please sleep on it for a while and let me know your
   answer.

▶ すぐにお答えできないので、少し考えさせてください。
- As I can't answer right now, let me sleep on it.

⑳返事は後日・検討は不要

■返事は後日

▶ 検討してあとでお返事します。
- I'll consider it and get back to you later.

▶ 調べてからお返事します。
- I'll look into that and get back to you.

▶ ちょっと考える必要があるので、明日ご連絡します。
- I'll get back to you tomorrow as I have to sleep on it.

▶ 今すぐお答えすることはできません。あとでお返事させてください。
- I can't give you an answer right now. Let me get back to you later.

▶ 数日後に明確にお答えできると思います。
- I'll be able to give you a definite answer in a few days.

■上司・本社と相談してから返事

▶ その件に関しては、本社と相談した上でお返事させていただきます。
- I'll get back to you on that after discussing with the head office.

▶ 上司に確認後、お返事させていただきます。

- Let me get back to you after I discuss it with my superior.

▶その件についてはまずはじめにチームメンバーと確認して、上司に相談する必要があります。

- I'll need to check with my team and discuss with my boss about that first.

▶ 社内で検討して可及的速やかにお返事します。

- We will consider it internally and get back to you ASAP (as soon as possible).

■これ以上の検討は不要

▶ これ以上検討する必要はありません。

- No further consideration is needed/necessary/required.
- There is no need to consider this further.
- There is no need for further discussion.

▶ この問題に関してこれ以上の作業（調査）は不要と思います。

- I think any further work (research) regarding/on this issue is unnecessary.

㉑根拠を示す

basis, foundation 基礎、根拠

evidence 証拠・裏付け

proof 証拠（決定的な、疑う余地のない）

reason 理由

* 根拠、立脚点を意味する ground（grounds）は、通常の会話
ではあまり使われないようです。

■ 根拠・理由は？

▶ どういう根拠があってそんなことを言うのですか？

- **On what grounds do you say that?**
- **Do you have any justification for saying that?**

▶ あなたの懸念には根拠があるのですか？
　（何を根拠に懸念されているのですか？）

- **Is there a basis for your concern?**

▶ 疑っているのには理由（根拠）があるはずです。

- **There must be a reason/basis for your suspicion.**

▶ そう考える理由はあるのですか？

- **Is there any reason for thinking so?**

■根拠・理由を説明

▶ なぜこれが最高のアイデアと思うのか、理由を説明しましょう。

• Let me give you the reason why I believe this is the best idea.

～の理由を説明します
Let me give you the reason why ～
I would like to show you why ～
The reason is that ～
The reason why ～

▶ 私が持っている具体的な根拠と、それを裏付ける論文をお見せしましょう。

• Let me show you the specific evidence I have and the papers that support it.

▶ これが我々が早急に開始すべき理由の一つです。

• This is one of the reasons why we should start ASAP.

▶ 意見は何らかの証拠やデータに裏付けられている必要があります。

• Opinions must be backed by/with some sort of evidence or data.

backed with, backed by は置き換え可能ですが、どちらかというと、backed by のほうがよく使われているようです。

㉒意見・コメントをはさむ

▶ どなたか意見はありますか？

- **Does anyone have something to say?**
- **Does anyone have an opinion?**

■他人の話を遮って自分の意見を述べる

口を挟む、話をさえぎる
interrupt, cut in, jump in　いずれも「割り込む」という意味

chime in「チャイムを鳴らして中にはいる」、話に割り込むというニュアンス

▶ ひと言いいですか？

- **Can I say a few words?**

▶ ちょっとだけよろしいですか？

「お話しを中断して申し訳ないですが、コメントしてもよろしいですか？」のニュアンス

- **Can I interrupt you for a moment?**
- **May/Can/Could I chime in (here)?**
- **Can I cut in?**
- **May I have a moment?**

▶ すみません。ちょっと発言してもよろしいですか？

- **Excuse me. May/Can/Could I (just) say something?**
- **Can/Could I say something?**
- **Can I add something?**

▶ 話しの邪魔をして申し訳ありませんが、コメントしてよいですか？

- Sorry to interrupt, but I'd like to comment on that.
- Excuse me for interrupting, but, may I say something?

■話が終わるまで待ってほしい

▶ すみません、おっしゃりたいことがあるのはわかります。ですが、私の話が終わるまでお待ちいただけますか。

- Excuse me, I understand you have something to say/add, but please wait until I've finished talking.

▶ 少しお待ちください。私の話が終わってからお聞きします。

- Just a moment, I'll hear what you've got to say after I'm done.

Coffee Break
― 口を挟まないで！（ケンカ腰ですので、ご注意！）

（ぶしつけに）話を遮る、割って入る
cut someone off (rudely)
干渉する、口出しする、介入する
butt in, interfere, intervene
私が話している時に口をはさまないでください。
- Please don't butt in while I'm talking!
- Will you please stop cutting in when I'm talking?
- Please don't cut me off before I finish talking.
- Please don't interrupt me until I finish speaking.
- Let me finish, please!

㉓指摘や批判に対処する

■質問の意図が理解できない

▶ すみませんが、あなたが何をおっしゃりたいのかよくわかりません。
- Sorry, I'm not sure I understand what you're getting at.
- I'm afraid I don't understand what you're trying to say.

▶ あなたの質問の意図（意味）がわかりません。
- I don't understand the intention/meaning of your question.

▶ すみませんが、全く理解できません。
- Sorry, but I'm completely lost.
  （話しに全くついて行けず、迷っている状態）

▶ 申し訳ありませんが、あなたの話についていけません。
  （あなたの言っていることが理解できません）
- I'm afraid I don't follow (you).
- I'm afraid I'm not following you.
- I'm afraid I'm not quite with you.

■もう少し具体的に話してほしい

▶ （質問内容を）もう少し具体的にお願いします。
- I'm sorry, but could you be more specific (with your question)?
- I'm sorry, but be (a little bit) more specific, please?

■言いたいことはわかるが〜

▶ おっしゃりたいことはわかりますが、完全には賛同できません。

- I understand your point, but I don't fully agree.

▶ 言いたいことはわかりますし、ある程度は同意しますが、完全に同意することはできません。

- I understand what you're getting at and I agree to a certain extent, but I cannot agree completely.

▶ おっしゃることはよくわかりますが、私のやり方はユニークな解決策だと思います。

- I understand your point, but I believe my approach offers a unique solution.

■良いご指摘とは思うが〜

▶ 良いご指摘と思いますが、[G]。

- I think you bring up some good points, but [G].

[G] に入れる言葉の例：

あなたは全体像を見失っていると思います	I think you're missing the whole picture
少し異論があります	I would like to make a small objection
私は事実と証拠を重く見ています	I take facts and evidence seriously
予算に限りがあることを忘れないでほしいです	I'd like to remind you that our budget is limited
私たちは観点が異なると思います	I think we have different perspectives/points of view

ひとつ言っておくべきことは、あなたの短期的効果と異なり、長期的な効果という点で私たちのアイデアがいかによく考え抜かれたものであるかということです。	one thing that's worth mentioning is how well thought out our idea is in terms of long-term effects unlike the short-term effects of yours.

■お言葉を返すようだが～

▶ お言葉を返すようですが、あなたの考えは現実的（実現可能）ではないと思います。

- **With all due respect, I don't think your idea is realistic/feasible.**
- **I understand what you're saying, but I don't think your idea is feasible.**

  "with all due respect" は、「大変失礼ながら」「お言葉に敬意を表するものの～」「はばかりながら」というニュアンスで、丁寧に反論するときの前置きとしてよく使われます。

  「お言葉ですが」のニュアンスとして、下記のような表現もあります。

  If you don't mind me saying so, ～
  I understand your point, but ～
  I'm sorry to contradict you, but ～
  I don't mean to contradict you, but ～
  I'm not trying to be rude, but ～

▶ そうとも言えるかもしれませんが、その逆もまたしかりです。

- **You could say that, but it's also true the other way round.**
- **You could say so, but it also works the other way round as well.**
- **You may be right, but the opposite is also true.**

■建設的な批判をしてほしい

▶ 他人を批判するのは簡単です。
- It's easy to criticize others.

▶ 建設的な批判をお願いします。
- Please give constructive criticism.

▶ 批判する場合は、建設的な批判をしてください。
- If you are going to criticize, please be constructive in your criticism.

▶ もし合意に至らず、意見の相違が続くようでしたら、解決策（代替案）の提示をお願いいたします。
- If we can't reach a consensus and keep disagreeing, please share your own solutions/alternative ideas on the matter.

Coffee Break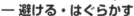
― 避ける・はぐらかす

問題や質問などを回避する
sidestep, avoid, dodge (the issue/question/problem)
質問をはぐらかす
sidestep/avoid/dodge a question
物議を醸すような（異論の多い）問題を避ける
sidestep a controversial issue

あなたは質問をはぐらかしています
- You're sidestepping the question.
sidestep の意味
① to step to the side in order to avoid something
② to avoid to talk about the specific issue, by starting to talk about something else.

㉔譲歩・妥協する

■譲歩する

▶ 解決に向けて双方がある程度の譲歩をした。

● Both sides made some concessions to reach a solution.

譲歩する	make a concession make concessions make some concessions
妥協する	compromise come to a compromise make a compromise
妥協に達する	reach a compromise
要求を受け入れる 譲歩する（折れる、応じる）	give in yield
少し譲ってお互いに妥協する （give in には負けを認める意味 もあります）	give in a little and compromise with each other
お互いに歩み寄る （中間地点で会う）	meet someone halfway meet each other halfway both sides meet halfway
融通がきく、柔軟である	be flexible

■妥協できる・妥協できない

▶ それが実現できるのであれば、多少の妥協は厭いません。

● I'm willing to make some compromises if we can get it done.

▶ あなたも妥協してくださるなら、私も喜んで妥協します。

- I'm willing to compromise if you're willing to as well.

▶ あなたがより良いアイデアを持っていらっしゃるなら、妥協する準備はできています。

- I'm ready to compromise if you have a better idea.

▶ 後々成功するためには、少し妥協する必要があります。

- In order to be successful later on, we will have to compromise a little.

▶ もう少し価格を妥協していただければ、注文を増やせるのですが。

- If you could compromise on price a bit, we would be able to increase our order.

▶ もちろん、注文量を増やしていただければ、喜んで妥協します。

- Sure, we're willing to compromise if you increase the order size/quantity.

▶ この件に関しては、残念ながら妥協できません。

- I'm afraid I can't compromise on this matter.

▶ 最小発注単位については多少の妥協はできますが、価格については残念ながら妥協できません。

- We can give in a little on the minimum order quantity, but unfortunately, we cannot compromise on the price.

■双方が歩み寄る・譲歩する

▶ お互いに譲歩しましょう。

• Let's meet each other halfway.

▶ この件でお互いに歩み寄ることはできませんか？

• Can't we meet halfway on this?

▶ うまく行くかどうかわかりませんが、私は最善を尽くしています。あなたも歩み寄っていただけますか？

• I'm not sure I can make this work, but I'm doing my best. Are you willing to meet me halfway?

▶ この件では双方が歩み寄ることを提案したいと思います。

• I would like to suggest that we meet halfway on this matter.

▶ 交渉でより良い条件を引き出すためには、少しだけ譲歩する必要があります。

• To get better terms in negotiations, you need to make small concessions.

■融通がきく（柔軟である）

▶ 顧客と交渉する時はもう少し融通をきかせるべきです。

• We should be a little more flexible when negotiating with our clients.

▶ 我々が競争力を維持し成功するためには、変化する業界のニーズに柔軟に対応することが極めて重要です。

• Being flexible to changing industry needs is crucial for us to stay competitive and successful.

㉕〜するよう説得する・説得力がある

説得する 　Ａ に〜するよう説得する	persuade 　persuade A to 〜
説得する、納得させる、確信させる 　Ａ に〜を納得させる	convince 　convince A to 〜
思いとどまらせる 　Ａ に〜しないよう説得する	dissuade 　dissuade A to 〜

＊ persuade は「相手に〜するよう説得する」ことで、相手が
納得しているかどうかは不問。
convince は相手に納得させ、確信させる（信じ込ませる）こと。

■どうすれば説得できるか

▶ どうすれば顧客に当社の製品を買ってもらえるでしょうか？

● **How can we persuade our customers to buy our products?**

▶ 新製品を購入してもらうためには、まず顧客との信頼関係を築く必要があると思います。

● **In order to persuade our clients to buy our new products, I believe we have to build trust with them first.**

▶ 新商品の価値をきちんと顧客へ説明できれば、納得して購入してもらえるでしょう。

● **If we can properly explain the value of our new products, we will be able to convince customers to buy it.**

▶ どうしたら顧客に当社の商品を納得して購入してもらえるか、4つの方法を考えてみました。

● I have come up with 4 ways to convince customers to purchase our products:

1. 製品に関する明確で具体的な説明	Provide clear and concrete descriptions of our products
2. 製品の差別化： 他社製品と比較したときの優位性と独自性	Product differentiation: Identifying the competitive advantage and uniqueness over other products
3. 価格面での優位性	Advantages in pricing
4. 安心の顧客サポート （どんなことでも気軽に問合せできるように）	Reliable and easy customer support (so that they can contact us easily regarding any inquiries)

■説得力がある

▶ 著名な科学者からのお墨付きは信じられないほど説得力があります。

● An endorsement from a renowned scientist is incredibly persuasive.

▶ 説得力のある発表原稿が書けるかどうかわかりませんが、とにかく最善を尽くして原稿案を作ります。

● I don't know if I can prepare a persuasive presentation script, but, I will do my best and prepare the draft anyway.

通常、script は演説やプレゼンなどの原稿、manuscript は本や論文などの出版予定の原稿。
プレゼンでは presentation script, speech notes が一般的。

㉖議論の余地はない・余地がある

■議論の余地はない・疑いの余地はない

▶ これは議論の余地のない事実です。

- This is an indisputable fact.

▶ これは疑いようのない事実です。

- This is an unquestionable fact.

  indisputable（議論の余地がない）と unquestionable（疑う余地のない）は類義語ですが、微妙に異なります。
  「異議を唱えたり反論できない」ことを強調したい場合は前者、「疑う余地がない」ことを強調したい場合は後者が適しています。日常的には unquestionable のほうが一般的に用いられ、indisputable は法律や科学などの学術的な文脈でよく使用されます。

▶ 喫煙が健康に良くないということは議論の余地がありません。

- It's indisputable that smoking is bad for your health.

▶ 彼女がその仕事に最適であることは疑いの余地がありません。

- It's unquestionable that she's the best person for the job.

▶ これは反論の余地のない（動かぬ）証拠です。

- This is irrefutable evidence/proof.

  「動かぬ証拠（決定的な証拠）」という意味で日常的には smoking gun がよく使われます。

▶ 本件については議論の余地はありません。

- There's no room for debate on this matter.

▶ これ以上 議論の余地はありません。

- There's no room for (further) argument (here).
- There's no room for further discussion.

▶ もはや議論の余地はないのではと思います。

• I think there's no longer any room for debate.

▶ あなたの意見を尊重しますが、この件に関しては議論の余地はありません。

• I respect your opinion, but there's no room for discussion (on this).

• I respect your point of view, but it's not open for debate.

■議論の余地がある

arguable, debatable, disputable, (be) open to debate

▶ これは議論の余地のある問題です。

• This is a debatable issue.

• This is a disputable question.

▶ 割引率については議論の余地があります。

• As for the discount rate, there's room for debate.

Coffee Break ☕
― 完璧にできたね！

You nailed it!

プレゼンは完璧だったね！

• You nailed the presentation!

あなたのスピーチは見事でした！
とても心温まる式典で、多くの人が感動して涙していました。

• You nailed the speech! (Your speech was amazing!)
  It was such a heart-warming ceremony, and many
  people were moved to tears.

㉗決断する・決断を促す

■迅速な決断を促す

▶ そろそろ決断しなければなりません。

• We have to make a decision fairly soon.

▶ 時間がなくなってきているので、早く決断していただけませんか？

• As time is running out/short, could you make a decision quickly?

▶ ～について速やかな決断をお願いします。

• Please make a speedy decision (about/on ～).

▶ あなた自身の判断に基づき、今すぐ決断することをお勧めします（コスト、利便性、競合、顧客の要望などの要素を考慮して）。

• We encourage you to make a decision now based on your own judgement (considering factors such as costs, convenience, competition, customer demand, etc).

■決断の前に徹底的な調査が必要

▶ 何かを決める前は必ず、物事を徹底的に調査する必要があります。

• Before you make any decision, you should always research things thoroughly.

▶ 苦渋の決断をせざるを得ませんでした。

- **I had to make a difficult/hard decision.**

■焦って決断しないように

▶ 焦って決断しないでください。

- **Don't rush into making a decision.**

決断するにはもう少し時間が必要だ。
I need some more time to make a decision.
急かさないでください。
Please don't pressure/rush me.
Please don't make me rush/hurry.

失敗しないよう時間をかけて取り組みたいのです。
I want to take my time, so that I won't fail.

▶ 感情的になって決断しないことが重要です。

- **It's important not to make decisions emotionally.**
- **You shouldn't allow emotions to dictate/influence decisions.**

感情が意志決定に影響を及ぼすことのないようにしましょう。
Do not let emotions affect decision-making.

感情的な意思決定は避けるべきです。
We should avoid emotional decision-making.

▶ 自分にとって正しいと思える決断を下すことをお勧めします。

- **We encourage you to make a decision that feels right for you.**

自分にとって正しいと思った方法で〜
自分に合った方法で〜
〜 in the way that feels right for you
〜 in a way that suits you

㉘多数決・挙手で決める・賛成・反対票を投じる

■多数決で決める

▶ 投票で決めましょう

- Let's take a vote.
- Let's decide by vote.
- Let's vote on it.

▶ 多数決で決めましょう

- Let's decide by majority vote.

  〜について採決する（多数決で決める）vote on 〜

  我々はこの提案に賛成7，反対2で採決した。
  We voted on the plan, with 7 in favor and 2 against.

▶ このトピックについては十分な議論ができたと思います。
  採決して、次の問題に移りましょう。

- I think we've had enough discussion on this topic.
  So, let's vote and move on to the next issue.

■挙手で採決する

▶ 挙手で採決したいと思います。

- I would like to vote by a show of hands.

  挙手による投票（採決）
  voting by a show of hands

  ➡ Coffee Break「賛成の人は手をあげて！」（p103 を参照）

■Zoom による採決方法

▶ Zoom で採決する方法について説明します。

- I will explain how to vote on Zoom (in a Zoom meeting).

▶ ご存知のように、Zoom では「挙手」機能があります。

- As you may be aware, Zoom provides a "raise your hand" feature.

▶ Zoom の「手を挙げる」機能を使えば、挙手した人数がホスト側に表示されるため、簡単に集計することができます。

- With Zoom's "raise your hand" feature, the number of people who raised their hands will be displayed on the host side, making it easy to count the number of hands raised.

■〜に賛成・反対票を投じる

▶ 彼は提案された決議案に賛成票を投じました。

- He voted in support of the proposed resolution.
- He voted in favor of the proposed resolution.

▶ 私はそれらの提案に反対票を投じました。

- I voted against those proposals.

■多数決で可決・否決する

▶ この提案は賛成多数で承認（可決）されました。

- This proposal was approved by a majority vote.

▶ この提案は反対多数で否決されました。

- This proposal was rejected by a large majority.

▶ 我々の大多数が提案された計画に賛成し、反対したのはわずか2名でした。

- The majority of us voted for the proposed plan and only 2 voted against.

㉙予測を立てる・予測を修正・調整する

■予測する・予測を立てる

予測する project, forecast, predict

これらは置き換え可能（interchangeable）なケースが多いようですが、実際にはニュアンスが微妙に異なります。

ビジネスや金融関係で使用される場合は projection、科学的な文脈において使用される場合は prediction がよく用いられます。

project （動） projection （名）	現在の状況や傾向、データに基づいて、将来のイベントや、収益、成長などを予測する。ビジネス、金融関係で使われることが多い。
	a projection focuses on a desired outcome （望ましい結果に焦点）
	a hypothetical outcome, or what might happen (in theory). 仮定的な結果、つまり（理論上）起こるかもしれないこと。
forecast （動、名）	多くの情報・データや科学的根拠に基づいて客観的に予測・予報する。天気予報や売上予測などに使われることが多い。
	a forecast focuses on most likely outcomes （最も可能性の高い結果に焦点）
	Forecast focuses on most likely outcomes/what you expect to happen, and is based on recent data, intentions, market, and trends. forecast は最近のデータ、意図、市場、トレンドに基づき、最も起こりそうな結果／起こると予想されることに焦点を当てています。

predict （動） prediction （名）	過去の経験や直感、情報などにもとづいて、予言・予想・予知・推測する。科学的または学術的な文脈において使われることが多い。 making educated guesses （経験則や直感、情報に基づいた推測）

■ Forecasts vs Projections

▶ 私達は将来起こるだろうことをデータや情報をもとに予想して予測を立てます。

• We prepare/make forecasts about what we expect to happen in the future, based on data and existing information.

▶ 一方、「What-if シナリオ分析」で将来起こる可能性を予測する時は projection が使われます。この場合、シナリオごとに予測は変化します。

• On the other hand, projection is used to predict the likelihood of future events in "what-if scenario analysis (WISA)". In this case, projections change under each scenario.

～について具体的な予測を立てる	make a specific projection about ～
できる限り正確な予測を立てる	make the projections as accurate as possible
現実的な／実現可能な予測を立てる	make realistic/feasible predictions/projections
合理的な売上予測を立てる	generate/develop/create a reasonable sales forecast

▶ これは我々が昨年立てた売上予測です。

- This is the sales projection/forecast we made last year.

▶ 実現可能な予測を立てる際には、実際の売上に影響を与えるすべての要因を考慮する必要があります。

- All factors that affect actual sales must be considered when developing a realistic forecast.

■予測できない

▶ 状況(事態)が落ち着くまでは何が起こるか予測できません。

- There's no way to predict what will happen until the situation calms down.
- It is impossible to make predictions until the matter calms down.
- No predictions can be made until everything settles down.

■予測を調整・修正する

▶ 私たちは予測を調整／修正する必要があります。

- We need to adjust/revise our projections.

▶ 私達は［H］に基づいて売上予測を調整／修正する必要が あります 。

• We need to adjust /modify our sales forecast based on [H].

［H］に入れる言葉の例：

需要	demand
変化する市場動向	the changing market trends
（入手可能な）最新情報	the latest (available) information
営業担当者からのフィードバック	feedback from the sales personnel
外部要因の変化	changes in external factors
ビジネス・ニーズの変化	changing business needs

▶ これは2年前に作成された5年間の予測ですので、大幅 に修正する必要があります。

• This is a five-year forecast prepared/made two years ago, so it needs to be revised significantly.

▶ 現在の販売不振は、予測を修正する必要があることを示 しています。

• The current weak sales indicates that we need to modify our projections.

▶ 予算が楽観的すぎたので（来年度の予算では）予測を調 整する必要があります。

• The budget was too overly optimistic, so we need to revise our forecasts (for next year's budget).

㉚〜を優先する・優先順位をつける

■〜を優先する

〜することが私たちの優先事項です	It is our priority to 〜 私たちの最優先事項は従業員にとって安全で健康的な環境を維持することです。 Our top priority is to maintain a safe and healthy environment for our employees.
〜を優先させる	make it a priority to 〜 工場は納期を守ることを優先させねばなりません。 Factories must make it a priority to meet deadlines.
〜を優先します	put/place a priority on 〜 私達はお客様のために高品質の製品を生産することを優先しています。 We put priority on producing high quality products for our customers.

▶ 品質を最優先にしよう。

- Let's make quality our top/highest priority.
- Let's put first priority on the quality of our products.

▶ 品質が我々の最優先事項です。

- Quality is our first priority.

▶ 安全を最優先しよう。

- Let's place top priority on safety.

▶ 顧客を見つけることを優先しよう。
- Let's put priority on finding clients.
- Let's make finding clients our priority.
- Let's make it a priority to find clients.

▶ 顧客の満足が当社の最優先事項です。
- The clients' satisfaction is our top priority.
- Our highest priority is customer satisfaction.

▶ 顧客との良好な関係を築くことが優先事項であるべきです。
- Having good customer relations should be a high priority.

▶ ウェブサイトに最新情報を掲載することが最優先されます。それをおろそかにしてはなりません。
- Keeping up-to-date information on our website is a top priority. We shouldn't neglect it.

■優先順位をつける

▶ 優先順位のリストを作りましょう。
- Let's make a list of priorities.

▶ 行動できる時間は限られているので、やるべきことに優先順位をつけましょう。
- We have limited time for action, so, let's prioritize what needs to be done.

▶ さあ、やるべきことに優先順位をつけましょう。
- Now, let's prioritize what we need to do.

▶ 優先順位を決めて上から順に進めましょう。細部については あとで考えればよい。

• Let's set priorities and proceed from the top. We can work out the details later.

Coffee Break
ー バズる

急速に拡散している、バズっている（インターネットや 口コミで）go viral（viral はウィルス virus の形容詞）

その情報はソーシャルメディア上で急速に拡散した。
• The information went viral on social media.

最近の騒動後、"○○○逮捕"というハッシュタグが 急速に広まった。
• "○○○ Arrested" hashtag went viral after the latest uproar.

もし適切に行えば、バイラル マーケティングは非常 に効果的で、コストもほとんどかからない。
• If done properly, viral marketing is very effective and costs almost nothing.

バズ マーケティングとバイラル マーケティングの 違いは、前者が企業側が積極的に関与して商品を 流行らせる戦略方法であるのに対し、後者は口コミ などで自然に拡散されるような仕組みを作るマーケ ティング手法であると言えます。
• The difference between buzz marketing and viral marketing is that the former is a strategic method in which the company is actively involved to make the product go viral, while the latter is a marketing method that creates a mechanism for the product to spread naturally by word of mouth.

㉛本題・計画などから逸れる

■本題から逸れる

▶ 本題から逸れてしまったので、戻しましょう。

- **We've gone off topic, so let's get back to it.**
- **We've deviated from the main topic, so let's get back on track.**

  すみません、話が逸れてしまいました。
  Sorry, I went off topic.
  Excuse me, I got off track.

  話が本題から逸れてきていると思います。
  I think we're getting off topic/track.
  I think we're deviating from the main topic.

■（計画などから）逸脱する

▶ 事業計画に沿って行きましょう。逸脱しないようにしてください。

- **Let's stick with/Follow the business plan. Please don't deviate from it.**

  （進むべき道から）逸脱する　deviate (from)

  計画から逸脱する　deviate from the plan

  スケジュールから外れる　deviate from a schedule

  彼は会社の目標から逸脱して自分の（好き勝手な）ことをやっている。
  He's deviating from the company's goal, and doing his own thing.

  自分のやりたいこと（好きなこと）をやる
  do one's own thing

㉜取り残した問題・検討を次回に持ち越す

■取り残した問題があれば〜

▶ ほぼすべてをカバーできたと思います。

- I believe we've covered almost everything.

▶ 重要な課題はすべてカバーしたと思いますが、もし取り残した問題（見落とし）があればお知らせください。

- I think we've covered all the important issues, but if there are any I've left out please let me know.
- I think we've covered everything on the agenda, but please let me know if we've missed anything.

省く、除外する、（説明などを）言い忘れる　leave out
見落とす、見逃す　miss out, overlook

■ほかに話しておくべきことは？

▶ ほかに話しておくべきこと（案件、懸案事項）はありますか？

- Is there anything else we should discuss?
- Is there any other business?
- Are there any outstanding issues?

その他の案件、その他の議題
any other business (AOB と略される)

懸案事項　concern(s), pending issue(s)

未解決の問題　outstanding issue(s)

▶ 時間がまだ少し余っています。何かこの場で話したい事はありますか？

• We still have some time left. Is there anything you'd like to discuss?

▶ もし時間が余れば、おそらくないと思いますが（笑）、私達の将来の計画をお見せしたいと思います。

• If we have some time left, which I don't think we will (hahaha), I would like to show you our future plan.

■次回に検討する

▶ その件につきましては、今日の議題に含まれていませんので、次回にしましょう。

• That issue/topic is not on today's agenda, so let's talk about it in the next meeting.

▶ この問題については次回に再検討しましょう。

• Let's revisit this issue next time.

Coffee Break
― 賛成の人は手をあげて！

to raise your hand, a show of hands

賛成の方は挙手をお願いします。
• All those in favor, raise your hand please.
• Let me ask for a show of hands for those who agree (with this idea).
• Can I have/get a show of hands for those who agree?

㉝全員が同じ認識を持つ

■全員が同じ認識をもつ

▶ 成功するためには全員が同じ認識を持たねばなりません。

- **To be successful, everyone must be on the same page.**

  認識が一致している、同じ考えを持っている、大筋で合意している
  on the same page

  "on the same page" の言い換え

  in agreement, having the same understanding/thoughts,
  of the same mind

▶ 目標達成のため、全員が同じ認識を持つようにしなければなりません。

- **To achieve our goals, we need to make sure everyone is on the same page.**

  "on the same page" については p54 を参照

Coffee Break
― その時が近づいたら

nearer the time, when it gets closer
when the time draws near, closer to the～

その日が近づいたら連絡しますね。
- **I will contact you when it gets closer.**
- **I will contact you nearer the time.**

詳細については、予定日が近づきましたらお知らせします。
- **We will provide more details when it gets closer to the scheduled date.**

その時期が近づいたら考えましょう（心配するのはまだ早いです）。
- **Let's worry about it when the time gets closer.**

㉞チャンスにかける

▶ チャンスだと思って（思い切って）やってみよう！

- Let's take a chance (and do it)!

▶ 我々に勝機はまだあります。

- There's still a chance for us to win.

▶ 我々がこの競争で成功する可能性は十分にあります。

- There is a good chance that we will succeed in this competition.

▶ もし [1] すれば成功する機会があるかもしれません。

- We may have a chance to be successful if [1].

    [1] に入れる言葉の例：

私達全員が自分の役割を果たす努力をすれば we all make the effort to do our part
顧客が何に価値を置いているのか理解できれば we understand what our customers value
顧客のニーズを正確に理解できれば we accurately understand our customers' needs

▶ 我々の製品をより高く売る機会があるかもしれません。

- We might have a chance to sell our product at a higher price.

▶ うまく行かない可能性はありますが、それを恐れていては何もできません。

- There is a possibility that it won't go well, but you can't do anything if you're afraid.

105

㉟成功の秘訣・困難な問題を克服

■成功の秘訣は〜にある

▶ 成功の秘訣は円滑で効果的なコミュニケーションにあります。

- The secret to success lies in smooth and effective communication.

▶ このプロジェクトを成功させる最も重要なことの一つは、顧客との効果的（良好、円滑）なコミュニケーションです。

- One of the most important things to make this project successful is having effective (good, smooth) communication with clients.

▶ プロジェクトの目標、目的、および望ましい結果（最終的に期待していること）を明確にすることが、成功への第一歩です。

- Defining the project's goals, objectives, and desired outcomes is the first step towards success.

  （意味、役割などを）明確にする　define 〜

■成長する可能性

▶ これは非常にリスクの高い試みですが、[J] 可能性を秘めていることも事実です。

- Although this is a very risky endeavor, it also has the potential [J].

［J］に入れる言葉の例：

長期的に大きく成長する	for significant long-term growth
大きな利益を生む	for significant benefits
大きな発展を遂げる	for significant development
医療界に多大なる影響を与える	to have a tremendous impact on the healthcare industry
効率を大幅に向上させる	to have a tremendous improvement in efficiency

■困難な問題を克服する

▶ この問題を克服できる可能性はあります。

• There's potential to overcome this problem.

▶ 我々は最も困難な部分（時期）を乗り越えられたと思っています。

• I believe we have overcome the most challenging part (period).

▶ 我々は最も困難な問題を克服しましたが、これからはプロセスを加速せねばなりません。

• We've overcome the most challenging issues, now we must speed up the process.

▶ 信じられないかもしれませんが、失敗は成功への第一歩です。

• Believe it or not, making mistakes is the first step to success.

信じようが信じまいが　believe it or not

㊱一丸となって頑張る

■一丸となって頑張ろう

▶ 我が社の存続をかけて一丸となって頑張ろう！

• **Let's work together as a team for the survival of our company!**

一丸となって働く
work as a team / work as a unit

団結する、力を合わせる
combine efforts
band together（一丸となる、結束する、団結する）
pull together（一緒にオールを漕ぐ➡団結する）

▶ 一致団結して頑張りましょう！

• **Let's work hard together.**
• **Let's work hard as one.**

▶ チーム一丸となって頑張りましょう！

• **Let's pull together as a team!**

▶ 皆で頑張っていきましょう！

• **Let's all hang tough!**

頑張れ！
Hang tough!, Hang in there!

彼は交渉相手から最大限の譲歩を引き出すために、粘り強く頑張っている。
He's hanging tough to extract the maximum concessions from his negotiating partner.

▶ 皆で乗り切りましょう！
- Let's get through this together!

▶ 力を合わせて実現させましょう！
- Let's team up to make it happen!

▶ 諦めずに頑張っていきましょう。
- Let's stick with it without giving up.

▶ 成功するためには一丸となってやる必要があります。
- We need to do it as one to be successful.

Coffee Break
— 最後まで聞いてよ！

聞いてよ！
- Listen to me！

最後まで聞いてよ！
- Hear me out！

私の話を最後まで聞いてください。
- Hear me out.
- You should at least hear me out.
- Will you hear me out?

私の話を最後まで聞いてから、（そのプランについて）あなたの考えを教えてください。
- Please hear me out and then tell me what you think (of the plan).

㊲総括する

■もう時間があまりない

▶ もう時間があまりありません。
- We're running out of time.
- We're short of time.
- Time is running short.
- There's not much time left.

▶ 予定より遅れています。
- We're behind schedule.
- We're running behind schedule.

■あとコメント１つで終了

▶ 残念ながら時間がもうありませんので、あと１つだけコメントを受け付けます。
- I'm afraid we're running out of time, so we can only accept one more comment.

▶ あとコメント１つ（ひと言）だけ、それで終わりにします。
- Only one more comment, then we need to finish.
- I'll just say one more thing, and that's it.
- One last thing before wrapping up (the meeting).

▶ それでは、今日話しあったことをまとめて終わりにしたいと思います。
- Now, I'd like to conclude with a summary of what we've discussed today.

■重要点をまとめる

summarize	重要点について要約する
recap (= recapitulate の短縮形)	話し合った内容の重要点をまとめる
review	おさらいする
go over	見直す、おさらいする、確認する

summarize = to make a short statement giving only the main information

recap = to repeat the main points of something that has been discussed

要約すると、まとめると
to sum it up, in summary, to summarize

▶ 今日の会議（議論の要点）をまとめましょう。

- Let's summarize today's meeting.
- Let me summarize the main points (of what we've discussed today).
- I'd like to summarize today's meeting.

▶ 重要点を簡単に総括しましょう。

- Let me briefly/quickly summarize the important/main key points.
- Let's recap today's meeting.

▶ 今日話しあった内容を簡潔におさらいしましょう。

- Let me briefly go over/review what we've covered today.

㊳閉会

■閉会する

閉会する close, finish, conclude, wrap up, end/stop here, call it a day/night

▶ そろそろ（閉会の）時間です。

- **Time's nearly up.**
- **Time to call it a day.**
- **That's all the time we have.**

▶ アジェンダはすべてカバーしましたね。

- **We've covered everything on the agenda.**
- **That covers everything.**

▶ これで今日の会議は終わりです。

- **That concludes today's meeting.**

▶ 終わりにしましょう。

- **Let's finish/end here.**
- **That's all for today.**
- **Let's wrap up the meeting.**
- **It's time to wrap up.**

Coffee Break
― 終わりよければ全てよし

All's well that ends well.

シェイクスピアの戯曲「All's well that ends well」のタイトルで、ことわざになっています。
会議の途中では喧々諤々（けんけんがくがく）の議論が展開されたとしても、「最後にうまくまとまれば、それでよし」ということですね！

下記のようなニュアンスを含んでいます。

wrap up	終わりにする、締めくくる
end here/stop here	まだやることはあるが、ここで終わりにする to stop at this point, even though there is more ここで昼食にして午後2時に再開しましょう。 We will stop/end here for lunch and resume at 2pm.
call it a day	その日の残りの仕事や活動を中断して家に帰ろう stop work/activity for the day and go home たいていは勤務時間が終わった(午後5時頃)か、疲れているか、やっていることがうまくいかず、イライラしているからのような理由。また明日頑張ろう。 Usually because work hours are finished (5pm), tired, or what you're doing isn't successful and you're frustrated. You'll try again tomorrow.
call it a night	仕事や活動を中断して寝よう stop work/activity and go to bed たいていは疲れていたり、時間が遅かったり、今やっていることがうまくいかないなどの理由で、明日またやろうと思う(残業、夕食会、コンピュータプログラミングなど) Usually because you're tired, it's late, or what you're doing isn't successful and you'll try again tomorrow (ex-overtime, dinner meetings, computer programming, etc.)

㊴参加のお礼・次回の会議について

■出席・貢献してくれたことへのお礼

▶ ご出席いただきありがとうございました。
• Thank you all for attending.

▶ ご貢献いただき、有難うございました。
• Thank you (all) for your contributions.

▶ 建設的なフィードバックをありがとうございました。
• Thank you all for your constructive feedback.

▶ 有益な情報をありがとうございました
• Thank you all for your helpful information.

▶ この分野における皆さんの経験とスキルは、計り知れないほど貴重なものです。
• Your experience and skills in this area have been invaluable.

▶ 最後に、ご参加いただいた皆様にお礼を申し上げます。
• Before I conclude, I'd like to thank you all for attending.

▶ 本日はお集まりいただきありがとうございました。またすぐにお会いできることを願っています。
• It was such a pleasure to have you here today and I hope I'll see you again soon.

■次回の会議について

▶ （念のためにお伝えしますが、）次回の会議は５月27日（火）
14時に予定されています。

- (As a reminder/Just a quick reminder,) the next
meeting is set up for Tuesday May 27th at 2pm.
- The next meeting is scheduled at 2pm on
Tuesday May 27th.

  忘れないようにお知らせしますが、念押しになりますが
  as a reminder, just a quick reminder

▶ 次回の会議は年内に開催予定です。

- The next meeting is scheduled to take place
before the end of this year.

▶ 次回の会合の日程について決まり次第、メールにてお知
らせいたします。

- We'll inform you of the next meeting via email
once the schedule has been decided.
- We'll email you as soon as the date and time for
the next meeting are decided/fixed.

▶ 最初に触れたように、議事録は１週間以内にメールでお
送りする予定です。
アクションプランや期日も含まれていますので、必ずチ
ェックしてください。

- As mentioned at the beginning, the minutes will
be emailed to you within a week.
It will include action plans with due dates, so
please be sure to check them out.

Coffee Break

― 炎上する（SNSで批判が殺到して炎上する）

（動）blow up, get flamed, get/receive backlash
（名）social media flaming
　　　flaming on X (Twitter)/YouTube/Instagram

SNS ではしばしば炎上することがあります。

- Flaming often occurs on SNS.

彼女のツイートが炎上した。

- Her tweet blew up.
- She received backlash on X (Twitter).

新キャンペーンを発信する際は、炎上して企業イメージを損なうことのないよう、言葉遣いに細心の注意を払う必要があります。

- When delivering our new campaign, we should be very careful to choose the correct wording so that it won't get flamed and damage our corporate image.

Coffee Break

― 細部まで気を配る（手を抜かない、慎重を期す）

dot the i's and cross the t's

「"i" に点を付け、"t" に横線を入れる」とは、「業務が完璧に行われるように、あらゆる細部に細心の注意を払う」、すなわち、i に点がきちんと入っているか、t に横線が入っているか、慎重に確認しよう、という意味で使われます。

= pays great attention to every small detail in a task, to make sure things are done completely
　より簡潔には carefully check all the details

この提案書を上司に見せる前に、あらゆる細部まで慎重にチェックする必要がある。

- We need to make sure that all the i's are dotted and the t's are crossed, before showing this proposal to our manager.

Coffee Break
― 点と点をつなぐ

connecting the dots

彼は点と点を解読して結びつける達人です。

• **He is a master of connecting the dots.**

スタンフォード大学の卒業式でスティーブ・ジョブズが行った伝説のスピーチの冒頭の言葉（日経新聞より引用）：

「世界でもっとも優秀な大学の卒業式に同席できて光栄です。私は大学を卒業したことがありません。実のところ、今日が人生でもっとも大学卒業に近づいた日です。本日は自分が生きてきた経験から、3 つの話をさせてください。たいしたことではない。たった 3 つです。まずは、**点と点をつなげる**、ということです。」

このスピーチに "**connecting the dots**" が何度も出てきます。全文が素晴らしく感動的です。

Stanford News（スピーチ動画）
"You've got to find what you love," Jobs says

https://news.stanford.edu/2005/06/12/youve-got-find-love-jobs-says/

ジョブズ氏スピーチ全訳 米スタンフォード大卒業式（2005 年 6 月）にて

日本経済新聞

https://www.nikkei.com/article/DGXZZO35455660Y1A001C1000000/

若い頃から日本の禅に傾倒し、日本人師匠に直接教えを受けるなどして日本の独自性や美的感性に多大な影響を受けたジョブズは、"Stay Hungry. Stay Foolish"「ハングリーであれ。愚か者であれ」という言葉でこのスピーチを締めくくっています。

Authors Profile

寺尾 和子 千葉大学薬学部卒業 薬剤師 英検1級

大手製薬企業（国内＆外資系）、大学病院薬剤部勤務等を経て、医学出版業界に転向（国際的医学出版社）。その後1997年に独立して小規模医学出版社 メディカル パースペクティブス（株）を設立。医薬品業界の情報誌（日・英二ヵ国語）を創刊し、ロンドンに英国オフィスを開設（1998～2008）。国際医学会議取材・医療記事の執筆のほか、一般書として『書きたい表現がすぐに見つかる英文メール』（共著）、『救済 マイケル・ジャクソン』（訳）、『ネイティブ表現が身につく英会話』（共著）などがある。健康増進のための医療関連の情報収集・分析と英語をライフワークとする傍ら、人に見捨てられた猫達の保護活動を日常としている。

柳川 史樹 薬剤師 薬学博士

薬剤師国家資格、薬学博士取得後、ハーバード大学―マサチューセッツ工科大(Harvard-MIT)共同健康科学技術部門へ研究留学。帰国後、日本企業による研究費 留学生賞をはじめ、研究助成のための様々な助成金取得プロジェクトに貢献。次世代の創薬技術開発および動物実験代替法*の確立を目指すべく、国立研究開発法人 産業技術総合研究所（産総研）にて特別研究員として、再生医療、組織工学、創薬研究等の研究に従事。その後、日本企業に転職し、米国での新規事業立ち上げに携わり、現在に至る（米国ボストン在住）。

*動物を使わずに、ヒトの細胞や組織などを用いて高度な技術を駆使して安全性や有効性等の試験を行う方法

クリステン・ラウンズ カナダ出身、結婚して米国ボストン在住、二児（娘）の母。心理学と人事管理を学んだのち、TEFL(Teaching English as a Foreign Language 外国語としての英語教師の資格）を取得、日本滞在中は英語教師としての経験を持つ。絵画、イラスト、グラフィックデザインなど、ビジュアルアートや応用美術に優れた才能を持つ。現在は育児に専念するかたわら、パートタイムで書籍や研究論文の編集を行い、自由時間には英語を教えている。音楽と動物を愛し、娘達が大きくなれば、まだ見ぬ景色を求めて家族旅行することを楽しみにしている。

Kristen Lowndes born in Canada, and now residing in Boston, is a happily married mother of two daughters. With a background in psychology and human resource management, she also holds an English teaching certificate (TEFL) and taught in Japan. Kristen possesses a remarkable talent for visual and applied arts, including drawing, illustration and graphic design.
Currently, she focuses on raising her girls while pursuing a part-time profession in manuscript editing for books and research papers. She enjoys teaching ESL in her free time, as well as indulging in her love for music and animals. As her girls grow older, she looks forward to traveling to new places as a family.

Other Contributers

柳川 真輝 制作およびマーケティング全般

稲岡 淳一 本文DTP

すぐに役立つ
オンライン会議のビジネス英語
★社内会議編★

発行日　2024 年 5 月 15 日　初版

著　者　　寺尾 和子／柳川 史樹
英文編集　　クリステン・ラウンズ
発行者　　柳川 真輝

発　行　　メディカル パースペクティブス株式会社
　　　　　〒215-0012　神奈川県川崎市麻生区東百合丘 3-26-1-403
　　　　　Tel: 044-978-1027　Fax: 044-978-1028
　　　　　https://www.med-perspectives.co.jp

印　刷　　欧文印刷株式会社

書きたい表現が
すぐに見つかる
英文メール

著者：アラン・フォレット／寺尾和子／上田素弘／寺澤恵美子

5 つの特徴

① イラスト満載！
② 見やすい！
③ 探している表現が
　すぐに見つかる！
④ 豊富な例文！
　（フォーマル&インフォーマル）
⑤ ひと口メモも役立つ！

定価 本体1900円＋税
ISBN978-4-944151-24-0 C2082

英語Eメールの書き方の書は数多く発行されている。しかしながら、いざ書こうとなると、自分が書きたいと思う表現が見つからない、という声を多く聞く。

　また、目上の人やビジネスに使用する丁寧語（フォーマル）とフレンドリー（インフォーマル）なメールの言葉の使い分けがわからないという声もよく耳にする。

　本書はこのような問題にできる限り対処すべく配慮して企画されたもので、豊富な例文と楽しいイラストが満載！英文メールを書く人の座右の書になること間違いない。

発行： メディカル パースペクティブス株式会社

『ネイティブ表現が身につく英会話』

［YouTubeでも音声が聞けるQRコード付］

Kristen J. Lowndes／寺尾 和子／寺澤 恵美子

定価 本体1650円＋税

● おしゃべり４人家族の日常会話

ネイティブ家族の自然な日常会話を学びながら『英語的な思考法』を身につけることを目標としています。登場人物は４歳の男の子、８歳のお姉ちゃん、ママ、パパのおしゃべり４人家族です。

● ボキャブラリー・ビルディングで広がる応用範囲

会話中に出てきた言葉について、その使い方や関連表現、類義語のニュアンスの違いなどを深く掘り下げて解説しています。今まで学校の授業で習ったことがないような、『そうだったのか！』と思わず頷くような説明が例文とともに掲載されています。

● 全頁カラー、日・英の吹き出し付きイラスト満載

絵本タッチで読みやすく楽しいイラスト満載で、飽きずに継続できるよう工夫されています。

● 音声 QR コード付・YouTube に公開

スマホやPCでネイティブの会話音声をいつでも聴くことができます（ダウンロード可）。